Praise for
Debt-Free U

"A real mule kick to the higher educational status quo. . . . He's a contrarian, and his book is packed with studies and statistics to back up his analysis. It's a magical combination that college-bound students and their parents should read."

—*USA Today*

"He has written the best and most troubling book ever about the college admissions process."

—Jay Mathews, *Washington Post*

"Provides a ton of food for thought for your college planning process."

—*Christian Science Monitor*

"Zac Bissonnette is one of the sharpest financial writers around. . . . Doogie Howser meets the boys from Facebook."

—Andrew Tobias, bestselling author of
The Only Investment Guide You'll Ever Need

"Let Zac Bissonnette help you plan for college, and you will finish rich."

—David Bach, #1 *New York Times* bestselling author of
The Automatic Millionaire and *Start Late, Finish Rich*

PORTFOLIO / PENGUIN

HOW TO BE RICHER, SMARTER, AND BETTER-LOOKING THAN YOUR PARENTS

Zac Bissonnette is an associate producer on the investigative team at CNBC. He has also written for the *Boston Globe*, the *Daily Beast*, the *Wall Street Journal*, *Glamour*, and the *New York Times Online*, and has appeared on CNN and the *Today* show. He has been featured in the *Washington Post*, *USA Today*, the *Wall Street Journal*, and *U.S. News & World Report*. Bissonnette graduated with an art history degree from the University of Massachusetts, Amherst, in 2011, and is a contributing editor with the *Antique Trader*.

HOW TO BE
RICHER, SMARTER,
AND BETTER-LOOKING
THAN YOUR PARENTS

Zac Bissonnette

PORTFOLIO / PENGUIN

PORTFOLIO / PENGUIN
Published by the Penguin Group
Penguin Group (USA) Inc., 375 Hudson Street, New York, New York 10014, U.S.A.
Penguin Group (Canada), 90 Eglinton Avenue East, Suite 700, Toronto, Ontario, Canada M4P 2Y3
(a division of Pearson Penguin Canada Inc.)
Penguin Books Ltd, 80 Strand, London WC2R 0RL, England
Penguin Ireland, 25 St Stephen's Green, Dublin 2, Ireland (a division of Penguin Books Ltd)
Penguin Group (Australia), 250 Camberwell Road, Camberwell, Victoria 3124, Australia
(a division of Pearson Australia Group Pty Ltd)
Penguin Books India Pvt Ltd, 11 Community Centre, Panchsheel Park, New Delhi - 110 017, India
Penguin Group (NZ), 67 Apollo Drive, Rosedale, Auckland 0632, New Zealand
(a division of Pearson New Zealand Ltd)
Penguin Books (South Africa) (Pty) Ltd, 24 Sturdee Avenue, Rosebank,
Johannesburg 2196, South Africa

Penguin Books Ltd, Registered Offices:
80 Strand, London WC2R 0RL, England

First published by Portfolio / Penguin 2012

1   3   5   7   9   10   8   6   4   2

LIBRARY OF CONGRESS CATALOGING IN PUBLICATION DATA
Bissonnette, Zac.
How to be richer, smarter, and better-looking than your parents / Zac Bissonnette.
p. cm.
Includes bibliographical references and index.
ISBN 978-1-59184-544-7
1. Young adults—Finance, Personal.   2. Wealth.   I. Title.
HG179.B5145 2012
332.0240084'2—dc23 2012001873

Printed in the United States of America
Set in Granjon
Designed by Alissa Amell

To my parents, who are actually wonderful—
and wonderful-looking *

And don't suffer the indignity of my spindly little legs

CONTENTS

With money in your pocket, you are wise and handsome, and you sing well, too.

—Yiddish proverb

HOW TO BE
RICHER, SMARTER,
AND BETTER-LOOKING
THAN YOUR PARENTS

Money, Power, and Really Broke Housewives

We must spend our money not merely for the adolescent and transitory things, but [for] this eternal, lasting thing that we call freedom.

—MARTIN LUTHER KING JR.

I remember being four years old, hiding out in the back storage room in our house, shivering and crying and clutching White Bear, wishing my parents would just stop yelling at each other. "Thank you for making my life an unmitigated misery," my mother shouted at my father, barely holding back the tears. Why was Mom so angry? Was he taking her on vacation to Branson, Missouri? Had he converted to Scientology? Or was she just hormonal?

No, as I continued to listen to the conversation, I learned what she was worried about: paying the bills.

This was my first lesson about money, and even though I know a lot more now, the one thing I did understand when I was four was that the reason my parents argued as often and loudly as they did was that they didn't have enough of it. My dad's construction business was in the red, and the modest salary my mother made as a therapist was not enough to pull us out of the hole.

My parents are both wonderful people, and I don't mean to

suggest that I had a miserable childhood. I had a great childhood. We grew up in a beautiful town on Cape Cod. We always had food. The lights never got turned off, and everybody loved one another—even though the constant financial stress eventually led my parents to divorce. When I look back on it, the elements of my childhood that *were* less than pleasant generally involved money. (And once when, at age seven, I was pantsed at summer camp.)

My dad taught me about money the way an alcoholic teaches his kids about drinking: by being a bad example. My dad is one of the most wonderful people I know. He was a hippie during the late sixties and early seventies, driving a Volkswagen bus with a bumper sticker that read, "No Left Turn Unstoned." At one point he actually lived in a tree house in a state park. When I was in middle school, he threatened to embarrass me by showing my friends pictures of his tree house. A skilled carpenter and in many ways a brilliant man, my dad has never liked to think about money and, consequently, doesn't manage it well.

This lifetime of financial inattentiveness culminated when I was in high school. He defaulted on his mortgage. While his friend, a lawyer, helped him work out a loan modification, he rented out his house and crashed at another friend's to save money.

One day, he and I got together to watch the Red Sox and a thought popped into my head.

"Dad," I asked him, "Who do you think thinks about money more? You or Bill Gates?"

"Without a doubt, me," he said and laughed. "I've spent my whole life trying to avoid thinking about money, thinking I was above it. Now it's all I can think about it. It's like money is exacting its revenge on me for ignoring it."

Money affects every aspect of our lives. When you have it, you can live the life you want and do things that make you truly happy; when you don't, every decision you make is based on what it will do to your finances. They say money is power, and it is. But I don't mean the greedy, control-the-world Donald Trump type of power; I mean the power to take control of your life without drama or stress about how you're going to make ends meet. Power is not about the car you drive, what percentage of your portfolio should be in bonds, or how to get the most airline miles; it's about freedom.

My parents' struggles with money formed the basis for my financial outlook—and managing my financial affairs better than my dad did has given me a peace in life that, as much as he deserved it, he never had. You may have had a similar experience—watching your parents struggle and hoping you never had to live through that kind of stress.

But this is the great thing—and why you are so smart to have picked up this book right now: You are at an age where developing a winning attitude about money, making a few smart decisions, and then automating them for the rest of your life (we'll get to that), can set you up for a lifetime of prosperous security far beyond what most of our parents have enjoyed.

And there's an added bonus: When you're on a financial game plan fueled by the knowledge and inspiration this book will give you, you will be able to very politely ask your parents to stop giving you advice.

The first rule of parenting is this: *Always dispense advice on everything, even if you have absolutely no basis for doing so*—like the time my sixty-three-year-old father told me I shouldn't lift weights because people wouldn't find me attractive if I added some muscle, even though, at a little under six feet, I only weighed about one hundred and forty pounds. The same is true for money. No matter how bad parents are with money, they still want to tell you how to manage it.

Take Lenny Dykstra. Dykstra was a star baseball player for the New York Mets and the Philadelphia Phillies from 1985 until 1996. He earned more than $36 million during that period, opened a chain of car washes, and emerged as an investment guru with frequent appearances on cable TV giving us kids financial advice.

Dykstra filed for bankruptcy in July 2009 with less than $50,000 in assets and somewhere between $10 million and $50 million in debt. By the next month, he was living out of his car and sleeping in hotel lobbies. Then he was charged with federal bankruptcy fraud and arrested for grand theft auto and possession of a controlled substance.

As Dykstra explained while his house was in foreclosure, "You pay your agent, you pay taxes, you buy the nice house, help the family out, and now you have, ya know, your dick in your hand, basically."

And yet—and this is where the first rule of parenting comes in—Dykstra is still providing his son Cutter, an unfortunately named second-round 2008 Milwaukee Brewers draft pick, with financial advice. When Cutter received a high six-figure signing bonus, he gave it to his dad to invest. According to the *New York Times*, Dykstra subsequently lost that money, too.

Hopefully, your parents are better off than Lenny, but if a guy who, by his own admission, made $36 million and ended up sleeping in his car is still proffering financial advice to his son, that means *nobody is safe*.

So the stakes are high, but the goal of this book is to help you, regardless of income or gender, end up with something even larger and more useful than Lenny Dykstra's dick in your hand at the end of each month.

Now, maybe you can't relate to Lenny Dykstra (perhaps because *you* weren't recently arrested and charged with placing ads for assistants on Craigslist and then exposing yourself to them when they showed up for the job interviews while you were awaiting trial on charges of drug possession, grand theft auto, and bankruptcy fraud). Perhaps the story of a young man I interviewed for a *Wall Street Journal* story is more relatable.

When Felipe Matos enrolled in college to study graphic design, he never thought the degree would be the very thing that prevented him from pursuing his dream career. But more than $50,000 in debt later, he found himself working as an assistant building manager—with half his salary going toward repayment of his student loans.

"In order to get into my field I'd have to intern," he explained, adding that his dream job would have been working in animation at Pixar. But in order to avoid defaulting on his loans—and the ruined credit and exploding compound interest that would ensue—he had to defer his dreams. And that was the easy part.

"I often get depressed because I always wanted to make cartoons and 3-D animations for a living but can't," he told me at the time. His debt load was also affecting the rest of his life, too. "I have a very loving and serious girlfriend," he said. "She doesn't care about my debt and believes in me but I'm afraid we can't have kids. . . ."

The point is this: Managing your financial life is not about spreadsheets and compound interest. It's about your *life*. The financial decisions you make can give you freedom or make you a slave.

The phrase "financial freedom" gets tossed around a lot, often accompanied by visions of hammocks on tropical islands. In fact, Amazon.com lists seven hundred and fifty books with that title. Three of the top-selling titans of the personal finance genre (Robert Kiyosaki, David Bach, and one of my favorite money writers of all time, Suze Orman) have all authored books with the words "financial freedom" in the title. But even without the hammock, it makes all the difference in the world.

Alli Mulder graduated debt-free from Indiana Wesleyan University five years ago in 2007. "After graduation, I didn't have to take any old job immediately just to pay my student loan bill," she told me. "The freedom of not having those payments has allowed me to put my money and my attention toward my dreams." Four years after graduating, she works as an enrollment counselor at her alma mater, where she helps other young people avoid the student loan trap.

These two stories show the contrast between financial freedom and debt bondage. Felipe and Alli earn about the same amount of money. But Alli is able to pursue the work that's important to her, while Felipe is chained to a job he hates. And satisfaction with one's career is a leading predictor of satisfaction with life, as we'll discuss in chapter 9.

Unfortunately, Felipe's story is far too common. One survey of corporate managers found that of the 68 percent of workers who said they would like to reduce the hours they spent working but couldn't afford to, more than half reported that their debt was holding them back.

Here are some of the ways money problems ruin people's lives:

People with high credit card debt are more likely to report high anxiety.[1]

People with high credit card debt are more likely to have physical health problems.

People with high debt are at increased risk for depression and even suicide.

Graduate students who reported higher debt in a survey were also more likely to report poor mental health and less satisfaction with life.[2]

An Associated Press poll found that 27 percent of people with high debt loads suffered from ulcers, compared with 8 percent of those polled who had low debt. Anxiety was 29 percent among debtors compared to 4 percent among non-debtors.[3]

And here's the tragic part of it: A weak financial life can cause so much stress that it impacts your work performance—and therefore your ability to improve your financial situation. Half the respondents of a poll conducted by Workplace Options said that their financial concerns cause them stress and anxiety; 48 percent of those respondents said the stress made it difficult to perform well at work.[4]

The importance of financial security has been known forever. The Bible has more than eight hundred mentions of money and property; *Jesus talked about money more than he talked about heaven and hell.*

It's a well-worn cliché (and so many clichés *are* well-worn, being *clichés*, after all) that money can't buy happiness. But as anyone who's suffered through a stack of unpaid bills will tell you, lack of money can be a one-way ticket to misery. I have a lofty hope: that this book will change the way you feel and think about money to bring you financial well-being, and a sense of security and peace in your life. That is what money, at its best, can provide.

This book contains no magic formula. There are no twelve-step plans, ten commandments, budgeting forms, checklists, songs, prayers, hieroglyphs, chants, bass lines, daily devotionals, journals, crop circles, or six-week makeovers. There are, however, strategies that will lead to happiness and success. And stories about the dumb things people do so you need not repeat them. You'll learn a lot about wine connoisseurs, Teresa Giudice, and how acting like the Internal Revenue Service can make you rich without any willpower. But mostly just Teresa Giudice. If you don't know who Teresa Giudice is yet, give yourself a pat on the back: You'll find out soon enough.

CHAPTER 1

Money Can't Buy Happiness
If You Spend It

Getting and spending, we lay waste our powers.

—WILLIAM WORDSWORTH

A few weeks ago I stumbled onto a copy of *The Real Housewives Get Personal*—a big, glossy, full-color guide to Bravo's hit series *The Real Housewives* that contains the secrets to money, success, fame, and glamour from the cast members of each of the spin-offs.

This wonderful $24.95 book was mine for $4.97 because it had been relegated to Walmart's Bargain Bin of Failed Books (proving that it actually *is* possible for businesses to lose money by underestimating the intelligence of the American consumer).

I bought the book (saving the receipt because, for a writer, research is a business expense), drove home, poured a stiff drink, and started reading. I ogled pictures of giant houses and lapped up all the housewives' secrets: their favorite restaurants, their favorite stores, their favorite cars, and the designer one of them uses for custommade $7,000 corsets. (People still wear corsets? *Soooo* nineteenth century.)

On page 107, along with pictures of New York City housewife

Alex McCord's $23,000 spending spree, was her explanation, "If you're going to consume, why not do it conspicuously?"

I'll tell you why: because as fabulous as these ladies may seem, you do *not* want to end up like them. Here are a few anecdotes about the housewives that somehow didn't make it into the book:

- NeNe Leakes, one of the stars of *The Real Housewives of Atlanta*, was kicked out of her five-bedroom apartment after a court ruled that she owed $6,240 in back rent. Her husband was reported to owe six figures in back taxes.
- Peggy Tanous of Orange County saw her house go into foreclosure. Yet the August 1, 2011, issue of *In Touch Weekly* (I read it so that you don't have to) reports that "Peggy, who has indulged in lip-fillers and a boob job, continues her monthly facials. She also still tools around in her Bentley and brags about how successful her husband is." Sounds to me as though the real boob job in this scenario is Mrs. Tanous.
- Gretchen Rossi, also of Orange County, lives on less than she once did—because her jobless boyfriend is $138,000 behind on child support.
- Taylor Armstrong, of Beverly Hills, had her credit card declined at Starbucks.
- Michaele Salahi of Washington, D.C., and her husband, now broke, have been sued seventeen times for issues involving their failed business ventures. Also, Salahi lied about having been a cheerleader for the Washington Redskins. If you were going to lie about being an NFL cheerleader, couldn't you pick a better team?
- Sheree Whitfield of Atlanta reportedly bounced a check for $386 that had been written to buy cake,[1] then had her Aston Martin repossessed because she owed her divorce lawyers $100,000. Could these events have happened on the same day? She went in to pick up the cake, was informed her check had bounced, and left the bakery as the tow truck was disappearing down the street?

- Orange County housewife Jeana Keough defaulted on her $1.3 million mortgage,[2] blaming the economy for her financial problems. I'd be more inclined to blame the fact that she had a $1.3 million mortgage.
- Atlanta housewife Lisa Wu-Hartwell, who is married to a professional football player, lost her $2.9 million home to foreclosure.[3]
- Alexis Bellino of Orange County fell behind on her $4.6 million mortgage, and was only able to keep the house because her lender agreed to a loan modification.[4] The house was worth so much less than Ms. Bellino owed there was no point in taking it back.
- New York housewife Sonja Tremont-Morgan filed for bankruptcy with debt of $19.8 million.[5]

This is an impressive list, but my all-time favorite is New Jersey's Teresa Giudice. She debuted on *The Real Housewives of New Jersey* as an extremely rich housewife married to a multimillionaire real estate developer. She was a stay-at-home mom who devoted her time to spray tanning, throwing lavish birthday parties, and, most memorably, flipping a table at a restaurant while shouting, "Prostitution whore!" at fellow housewife Danielle Staub. Her world came crashing down when she and her husband filed for Chapter 11 bankruptcy, reporting debt of more than $11 million against a monthly income of $16,500. The $16,500 actually included her fees for appearing on her terrible television show (yes, the "real housewives," who flaunt their wealth, are paid to be on the show), along with, get this, financial assistance from her family. Yes, the real housewife and her self-proclaimed self-made husband depend on relatives to support their lifestyle. This was the woman who once screamed at her sister for bringing store-brand cookies to a party: "Next time, you bring pignoli." For those of you who don't know what pignoli are . . . I'm sorry to leave you in the lurch, but I just don't care enough to look it up.

Believe it or not, there are even more of these stories and, by the time you read this, there will doubtless be more still. But you get the point. Executive producer Andy Cohen often refers to *The Real Housewives* franchise as a "sociology of the rich"—but it's one that features a bunch of broke people. This leads one to ask: What is the definition of wealth? A huge part of becoming wealthy is understanding and internalizing the benefits of wealth—and not getting caught up in stuff that looks like wealth but actually has nothing to do with it, like $7,000 corsets. No matter how much student loan debt you have—or how little savings—you are doing better financially than many of the "richest" people on television.

In August 2011, Spencer Pratt and Heidi Montag, the former stars of MTV's *The Hills*, made a startling confession to the *Daily Beast*: They were *broke*.[6] They'd blown through millions of dollars on everything from nose jobs to butt implants to chin augmentation to . . . OK, so they spent a lot on plastic surgery.

But they also spent a lot on clothes. "I probably spent a million dollars on suits and fancy clothes," Spencer said. "My whole million-dollar wardrobe—I would never wear that again. They're props. Everything we were doing, we were buying props."

Think about that: These two kids bought butt implants and suits they have no reason for wearing because they thought it would give them status—make them look better and feel better and therefore be better, but now they're just penniless and miserable.

A house you can't afford can be a prop. Or a car. Or a watch. When you think about it, we spend a lot money on props—stuff that makes us look like something we're not.

I started the research for this book with one simple question in mind: What should young people do with their money in order to have the best life possible today and for the rest of their life? After a year reading everything from the Bible to a nineteenth-century home-economics book that suggested using earwax as a free replacement for lip balm (seriously), I'm pretty sure I've found the answer: *You shouldn't spend it. On anything. Ever.*

OK, that's not entirely true, but it has been shown that spending money on stuff does not make you happier. Knox College psychologist Tim Kasser surveyed thousands of people, asking them questions about how interested they were in acquiring goods, how much they were concerned about how they were perceived by other people, and how happy they were. He reported that "the more materialistic values are at the center of our lives, the more our quality of life is diminished."

Dr. Kasser is not alone in his conclusions. Lisa Ryan and Suzanne Dziurawiec surveyed people in Australia and found that those who were most materialistic were "less satisfied with life as a whole."[7]

I'm telling you this not because I want you to feel bad that you've been saving for six months to own a pair of Jimmy Choos. I'm telling you this because understanding *why* you make decisions—especially when it comes to money—is the first step to making them better. If you're going into debt to buy something you think will make you cooler, not only will you be broke, you'll be terribly unhappy to learn that "having stuff" doesn't make you happy.

Consider the research:

- Princeton economist Angus Deaton and psychologist Daniel Kahneman found that the ability of income to increase happiness capped out at $75,000 per year. After that, increasing income stops making you happier.[8]
- Psychologist Ed Diener surveyed members of the Forbes 400. His findings? The four hundred richest people in America are not discernibly happier than the rest of us.[9] (Isn't that great?)
- Deiner and his fellow psychologist David Myers write that "people have not become happier over time as their cultures have become more affluent. Even though Americans earn twice as much in today's dollars as they did in 1957, the proportion of those telling surveyors . . . that they are 'very happy' has declined from 35 to 29 percent. . . . Those [individuals] whose income has increased over a ten-year period are not happier than those whose income is stagnant."[10]

- Dr. Thomas J. Stanley, author of *Stop Acting Rich*, surveyed people based on their brand of watch and asked them to measure their overall satisfaction with life on a five-point scale. There was no statistically significant difference in levels of happiness among people wearing Rolex, Seiko, or Timex.

It turns out that the ability to purchase luxury goods—or travel extensively or participate in expensive sports like water polo—does not lead to any increase in happiness at all. When we couple this fact with the statistics in the introduction about how debt can lead to severe depression, we find that the biggest factor that determines personal happiness is not whether you are wealthy, but whether your financial situation adds stress to—or subtracts stress from—your life.

One of my favorite stories about the meaning of "enough" comes from two great American fiction writers: Kurt Vonnegut and Joseph Heller. One evening, the two were at the party of a well-known hedge fund manager, whose haughty demeanor and pretentiousness inspired Vonnegut to ask Heller, "Joe, doesn't it bother you that this guy makes more in a day than you ever made from *Catch-22*?"

"No, not really," Heller said. "I have something that he doesn't have: I know the meaning of enough. I have far more than enough."

Enough. Think about that word and what it means to you. My hope is that you'll realize that what will bring lasting happiness to your life is a sense of peace that comes from knowing you have a plan, that you have some measure of security—*that's* what money can do.

Your TV Will Make You Poorer, Dumber, and Fatter Than Your Parents

Sadly, too many young people have grown up in a consumerist world that values "stuff" rather than one that values "enough." As a result, they're actually spending *more* money than the truly wealthy. A *Wall Street Journal* headline from January 2011 entitled "Who's Buying All

That Luxury? Not the Rich" reported on a study that showed that while the rich have cut back spending on luxury goods, lower-income Gen Yers have been leading the recovery in luxury goods sales. And going into credit card debt to do it.[11] Actual rich people had declined from 68 percent of luxury spending to just 38 percent. Most luxury spending in America is now done by non-rich people.

One reason we've gotten so profligate is that we've been exposed for our entire lives to examples of lavish consumption—whether responsible or not. Thanks in large part to reality television, especially our favorite *Housewives*, we're bombarded with the message that spending equals success. In fact, according to one study, the more television you watch, the more materialistic you tend to become and the more distorted your perception of reality. Consumer researchers Thomas O'Guinn and L. J. Shrum found that the more television people watch, the higher percentage of Americans they think have tennis courts, luxury cars, maids, and swimming pools. A Merck Family Fund poll found that the more debt people had, the more likely they were to admit that they "watch too much TV."

Thankfully, other research suggests that consumers can become less materialistic by simply watching less television and reminding themselves that affluent lifestyles portrayed on TV shows don't represent reality.[12]

If you love reality television and can't bear to turn away from those train wrecks, balance your viewing by following shows and websites that expose television personalities for what they are; so if you're going to watch *Bridezillas*, you should also watch *Chelsea Lately*.

Or you could just get rid of your TV. In her book *Money Secrets of the Amish*, an exploration of the financial acumen of the Pennsylvania Dutch, journalist Lorilee Craker suggests that their lack of televisions is a major contributor toward Amish families' renowned ability to build wealth—and keep it: "The Amish really do have an advantage by not having televisions," she writes. "They don't have to constantly deflect marketing messages targeted directly at their off-spring the way we do."[13]

I don't own a television; I haven't had one since my dad smashed his with a sledge hammer after a presidential election many years ago didn't go the way he'd hoped. But I'm not going to make fun of you (much) if you decide to keep yours. If you do want to wean yourself though, consider starting by simply monitoring how much you watch each week. Then try to decrease it by 10 percent. In another month, try cutting it by 10 percent again. I'll bet you'll find that your life improves as you cut back. At the very least, maybe you'll find time to read more of this book, which will definitely improve your life.

$999 iPhone Apps, Teresa Giudice, and the Dalai Lama

In 2008, an enterprising software developer created a $999 iPhone app that did nothing except flash the words "I Am Rich" across the screen.

Apple quickly canned the app though they didn't say why. But eight people had already purchased it.[14]

This is an extreme case of the stupid things people spend money on: It accomplishes absolutely nothing other than to signal to the world that you have money. My friend Jeff Yeager, who wrote a won-derful book called *The Cheapskate Next Door*, has an odd twist on the age-old question of whether a tree falling in the forest makes a sound if no one is around to hear it: "If you had a Ferrari and no one could see you driving it, would you still want it?"

Psychologists who have studied happiness and values divide the world into two broad categories of motivation: extrinsic and intrinsic. Extrinsic motivations come from outside the individual (through things like wealth, prestige, image, and possessions), whereas the in-trinsic come from within (curiosity, self-discovery, and a desire to impact the world in a positive way).

On average, people who exhibit primarily intrinsic motivations are likely to be happier. Under this reasoning, one can assume the Dalai Lama, who values things like inner peace and introspection, is more content with life than Teresa Giudice, who values pignoli cookies. But I'd venture to guess that even Teresa Giudice is more content than any of those eight idiots who spent $999 on an iPhone app.

Though, to be fair, ever since Mrs. Giudice stumbled into her financial woes, she's come to understand the importance of intrinsic motivation. In an interview she gave with *In Touch Weekly*, she said, "I'm terrified of being poor. I don't try to keep up with the Joneses anymore. I spend within my means."

She also said that instead of lavishing her daughters with the extrinsic trappings of luxury, she's focused on their long-term well-being and the power that financial freedom really can provide. She's started college funds for them and seems to be genuinely inspired to do so out of a desire to see her children succeed. "I want them to go to college and have careers so that they never have to rely on a man," she said.

Just as intrinsic motivation is more likely to lead to happiness than extrinsic motivation, using money to fulfill intrinsically oriented needs and interests is more likely to lead to happiness than using money to fill extrinsically oriented desires. That's why people who drive luxury cars aren't happier than people who drive non-luxury cars, but people who play music are likely to be happier than people who don't.[15]

Another study conducted by marketing researchers Marsha Richins and Scott Dawson found that the more likely people were to believe that possessions and wealth lead to happiness, the more likely they were to be unhappy and dissatisfied with their lives. They were also less likely to report having "fun."

In other words, not only does a focus on the outer trappings of financial success not lead to happiness but also thinking that it does leads to misery.

The safety and security that come from a stable financial life lead to contentment. Money can't buy happiness if you spend it. The best way to understand money and the role it should play in our lives is to look at the "hierarchy of needs" created by psychologist Abraham Maslow in 1943. Basically, the hierarchy of needs is a pyramid, with the most basic human needs—physiological (food, water, sleep) and safety—at the bottom and the more elevated, elusive ones—love and belonging, self-esteem, and self-actualization—at the top. If you want to see this as a visual, visit tinyurl.com/Zac-Maslow.

What does the hierarchy of needs have to do with money? Money beautifully meets the lower needs, like food and security. An emergency fund with a few thousand dollars in it can reduce the stress of an unexpected expense. But money less reliably meets the upper needs— like self-esteem and belonging. And when you overextend yourself trying to use money to meet the upper needs, you can find yourself foreclosed upon, your car repossessed, struggling to meet the lower needs, and so the whole thing collapses.

So how can you resist the temptation to use money to try to meet the upper levels of the hierarchy? Ah, glad you asked.

How to Fight Consumerism

Knox College psychology professor Tim Kasser gives his students possibly the most annoying assignment in the history of college. He instructs them to count how many ads they see for a week. Dr. Kasser told me that students who do this are "angry" by the end of the assignment—and not just because their professor had assigned them an impossibly time-consuming task in the first week of an intro-level course (although they're probably angry about that, too). His students are angry because they realize that people were constantly trying to manipulate them. But the exercise did make them more aware of— and therefore less susceptible to—the messages of consumerism and materialism.

Saving money doesn't sound like as much fun as spending it, so as you experiment with combating materialism, here are some ways to make it fun:

Make fun of advertising—or at least watch it consciously. According to Dr. Kasser, concentrating on advertising while you're watching it can serve to reduce—or even nullify—its effectiveness in terms of increasing materialism. "It's when you pay attention to the message that you realize it's silly," he says. Ads suggesting that you need to buy your girlfriend expensive jewelry in order to have a successful relationship (this is the premise of virtually every ad for jewelry that you will ever see) are obviously absurd. But if you aren't paying attention when you see them—and you're exposed to them over and over again—you start to subconsciously believe the messages, according to Dr. Kasser.

Play the product placement drinking game. With the advent of TiVo, it's easy to fast-forward through commercials. So the TV industry has started relying on record amounts of product placement, especially in reality shows. But it's bad in sitcoms, too. On an episode of *30 Rock*, Tina Fey prattles on about the benefits of Verizon cell phones and then stares into the camera and asks "Can we have our money now?" So have fun. Next time you're watching *Jersey Shore*, take a shot of tequila every time you notice an instance of product placement. I played this gmae wile I wrrrrrrrroet his sceot-ino nad ti aws fuuuuuuuuuuuuuunnnnnnnnnnnnnnnnn. My editor insists that I add the following note for legal reasons: You actually should not do shots of tequila while watching *Jersey Shore*. Another disclaimer: You should not watch *Jersey Shore*.

Ask yourself why you want to buy something. We've all heard the lectures about differentiating between wants and needs, so I won't bore you with another. But think of it this way: Every time we buy something, we do so to fill some kind of void in our lives. We spend based on the belief, in that moment, that our life will be a bit fuller with that item. This leads to bad impulse buys. Make a list of the things you most want to buy—you can include crazy dream items (like your own island) and more immediately within-reach splurges (like a new phone) and ask yourself, "What desire in my life am I hoping to fill with this purchase and is there a better, cheaper way of filling it?"

Picture yourself dead. OK so, admittedly, this is a bit creepy. But research shows that being aware of your own mortality—and asking yourself whether the way you're spending your time and energy is the way you want to live your own life—can help you make better decisions.

Cultivate nonmaterialistic hobbies and interests. Dr. Kasser says that focusing energy on hobbies and pursuits that don't promote materialistic values can help divert that impulse within us—and, by extension, make us better with our money. Painting, biking, yoga, meditation, iPhone Scrabble, chess—anything that involves focus and effort but doesn't cost a lot of money or feed the materialistic impulse will actually improve your financial life.

This is one of the reasons the Amish are so good with money. Their entire community and social network is structured around nonmaterialistic values. I don't expect you to move to a thatched-roof compound and grow your own cabbage—*or do I?*—but developing a community of friends who share an interest in nonmaterialistic pursuits is a great way to improve your financial life.

Gardening is a great example. In addition to being a great, character-building activity, this is something that can potentially save you a ton of money. According to a report released by Burpee, one of America's leading sellers of gardening supplies, families earn an average return of $25 for every $1 they spend on their gardens. That means if you put $200 into growing your own garden, you can save $5,000 per year on grocery bills.[16] Admittedly, this estimate comes from Burpee, world's largest seller of seeds. But even if it's significantly exaggerated, there's this: The time you spend in the garden is time that can't be spent shopping. (During World War I, the federal government's National War Garden Commission aggressively marketed gardening as a way to provide food for domestic needs—so that the food grown on America's farms could be sent abroad to feed the troops. Families could then buy war bonds with the money they saved on asparagus.) For help getting started, visit GCAmerica.org or pick up *Vegetable Gardening for Dummies* at the library.

Consider this list. Lorilee Craker, the author of *Money Secrets of the Amish* (and coauthor of Britney Spears's mother's autobiography, which means I automatically believe anything she says), wanted to "de-spoil" her children. She created a six-part plan to make her kids better with money, and I think it's a wonderful blueprint to try to put in place in our own lives:[17]

1. Teach them contentment with what they already have.
2. Show them how to hunt out savings and freebies.
3. Help them distinguish between wants and needs.
4. Say no with some regularity.
5. Encourage delayed gratification.
6. Teach them that hard work won't harm them, and is probably really, really good for them.

Why Thrift Will Make You Happier

Money's easy to make. . . . But with few exceptions people don't
want money. They want luxury, love, admiration.

—JOHN STEINBECK

In addition to materialism, another leading cause of financial diffi-
culties is inattentiveness: not paying attention to financial decisions,
floating through life overspending out of sheer laziness. In short, not
being thrifty.

Unfortunately, thrift gets a bad rap these days. It's seen as a
means to an end—a sacrifice you make today so you don't have to
sacrifice later on. Drive a crappy Honda Civic so that, when you're
ninety-four, you'll be able to buy a Lexus. But back in the day, thrift
was actually seen as an end in itself, and people believed that being a
good steward of resources was the key to a good life in both the short
term and the long term. In her thought-provoking book *Peace and
Plenty: Finding Your Path to Financial Serenity*, Sarah Ban Breathnach
writes that "the earliest meaning of the word thrift was 'the condition
of one who thrives' or being endowed with good luck, good fortune,
wealth, and health. But what made thrift such an honorable aspira-
tion was that its bounty was not conveyed by the celestial benediction
or favor of the Crown—but rather through the everyday choices
made by prudent housewives who were neat, clean, industrious,
imaginative, clever, enterprising, and generous."

Think about those adjectives. Those are *the* key words for a good
financial life: neat, clean, industrious, imaginative, clever, enterprising, and generous. The title of one study out of Utah State University
is even more interesting: "Bank On It: Thrifty Couples Are the Happiest." That study found that thriftiness correlated with happier,
more successful relationships. Other studies have found that thrift is
associated with higher self-esteem, better health, and less interper-

sonal conflict (studies Charles Dickens should have come up with before he created the character of Scrooge).

Breathnach sold seven million copies of *Simple Abundance* before losing all her money and writing *Peace and Plenty*. "We're given the stewardship over our lives," she told me. "The word thrift was the right apportionment of energy toward all of life. It wasn't parsimonious and it wasn't frugal and it wasn't cheap. Thrift is a rich word."

In the end, thrift is really about self-control: making conscious, thoughtful decisions about how to apportion your energy. Not only will it make you feel powerful to practice it with even the most minor purchases in your life, but also you'll actually end up more successful than people who don't. In 1972, Stanford psychologist Walter Mischel offered children between the ages of four and six a marshmallow, but told them if they waited fifteen minutes, they could have a second marshmallow, too. The children devised all sorts of tactics to avoid eating the marshmallow. According to Mischel, some elected to "cover their eyes with their hands or turn around so that they can't see the tray, others start kicking the desk, or tug on their pigtails, or stroke the marshmallow as if it were a tiny stuffed animal." Two-thirds ended up just eating the marshmallow.

When researchers followed up with the subjects more than a decade later, they found a significant correlation between the willingness to delay gratification and success in life. According to the report, "Preschool children who delayed gratification longer in the self-imposed delay paradigm, were described more than ten years later by their parents as adolescents who were significantly more competent." The ones who waited the full fifteen minutes ended up scoring 210 points higher on the SAT than the ones who ate the marshmallow immediately. (They were also less likely to be overweight—even though they had once upon a time eaten two marshmallows instead of one.)

Learning to say no to yourself—because you know that a better life with more marshmallows awaits you—is a key to a successful financial life, and a successful life generally. As psychologist Roy Baumeister and *New York Times* columnist John Tierney put it in their book *Willpower: Rediscovering the Greatest Human Strength*, "Ultimately, self-control lets you relax because it removes stress and enables you to conserve willpower for the important challenges."[18]

Slaying the Entitlement Dragon

But it's hard to say no. We live in an "I deserve it" bubble. Everyone thinks they deserve everything. One of my favorite comedians, Louis C.K., summed this up perfectly by describing a plane passenger's angry reaction when the wireless Internet stopped working. "This is bulls***!" the man exclaimed. "How quickly the world owes him something that he knew existed only five minutes ago," Louis retorted. This is entitlement in action, and it's one of the root causes of our financial problems.

All that self-esteem stuff from elementary school has caused people to believe that not only do they want cool stuff, but also they *deserve* it. Take this snippet from a 2009 *Boston Globe* article about Samantha Barbosa, a Boston University student who chose to pay $13,000 a year—$5,000 more than she would have paid for standard housing—for a room in a new luxury dorm on campus:

> "I applied by myself because my friends were all too cheap to live here," said Barbosa, who is paying for the room with student loans. "For the past three years, I lived in the lowest-priced dorms. Being a senior, I've worked really hard and I figured I deserve to live in a place like this."[19]

Does this girl have any idea what a complete loser she sounds like? She's living alone because her friends were "too cheap" to borrow an extra $5,000 to stay in an upscale dorm? Maybe her friends just wanted to live with people who are smarter than she is.

Here's the deal: If you don't have any money to buy some luxury good, then you don't deserve it. Everyone on the planet deserves food, but there are plenty of people in Third World countries who don't have it because they can't afford it. If there is no universal life force that entitles people to food, there certainly isn't one that entitles you to an iPad or hardwood floors. Color me coldhearted.

Here's something I started doing recently and, believe it or not, it's actually kind of fun. Every day, I say no to myself at least once. And I don't mean no in the sense of saying no to huge expenses I can't possibly afford but no in terms of more minor things that I would like to have but don't need: no to magazines in the grocery store that have Britney on the cover, no to that "Does 'Anal-Retentive' Have a Hyphen?" T-shirt I thought was funny.

Make a game out of it; see how many times you can say no to yourself today, and then try to do at least that, well, almost *every* day.

OK, so we have the basic framework laid out: Recognize that *stuff* doesn't lead to happiness, but that a willingness to say no does. The greatest thing you can do with money to increase your happiness is build a secure financial platform. I want to help you stop worrying about the uses of money that generate little if any return in terms of happiness—and instead use your money to generate the happiest life you can possibly have, now and forever. Sound good?

Then let's get into the specifics.

CHAPTER 2

The Financial Services Industry and You (Brought to You by the National Center for Domestic Abuse Prevention)

> What is good for the financial industry is bad for you.
>
> —JOHN BOGLE[1]

There comes a time in the life of almost every young man when he realizes that he's probably not going to make it to the National Football League, that his parents don't know *everything*, and that Tyra Banks's hair is not all hers. Although it is hers in the sense of "It's my hair, I bought it!" But still, we all have to accept that it is not real hair.

Here's another eye-opener: The world of banking, mutual funds, credit cards, and insurance is a world of greed, manipulation, and lies.

The quote from Jack Bogle above should be the mantra for your adventures in the financial world. It's not that bankers and financial advisers are bad people. Many of them are honest, hardworking, good people who put the interests of their clients first. However, the ones *you* meet will in all too great a likelihood not be like this.

The problem is that financial services professionals try to portray themselves as your friends: they're well mannered, well dressed, and well-spoken, and they seem to want to help you. But in reality they're the kind of people who will break into your house in the middle of the night and rape you—though the better ones will tidy up before they leave.

Here's the deal: The financial services industry, I'm sorry to say this, can't really create anything. Anyone reading this who works in the financial services industry is, of course, the exception. But in general, wealth is created by the employees of the businesses whose shares are *traded* on the stock market and whose bonds pay interest. Everything else is an illusion, with the gains ("I made $500 investing in shares of Citigroup before the economy tanked!" says your friend) being wiped out by the losses ("I lost $500 investing in shares of Citigroup before the economy tanked," says your other friend; except that he doesn't say that because rule number one of talking about stock investments at cocktail parties is that you must only mention your winners and rule number two is to exaggerate them).

It's the same with everything in the world of financial services. The only way that the credit card company can make money is for you to pay them a bunch of fees in exchange for giving you absolutely nothing. The insurer makes money by charging you premiums and then paying out less in claims than you paid in. They are playing poker with a marked deck. You may need a credit card (although you probably don't) or insurance anyway, of course, but neither one is creating wealth.

This dynamic is unique to the financial world. A bakery might charge you three dollars for a muffin that only cost them thirty five cents to make, but *you got a muffin*. In a business that does nothing other than exchange money—for money and nothing else—the only way for the financial industry to do well is to charge you more money than it ends up giving you back. I'm sorry that this is how the world works, just as I'm sorry Tyra's hair is not her real hair.

As you go through the financial world—whether banking, investing, insurance, or credit cards—your mission should be this:

Give those people as little of your money as you possibly can. There are a few exceptions to this rule but, in general, lower fees are almost always better, and don't let anyone BS you into thinking otherwise. Also, steal at least ten pens every time you're at a bank. (I trust you know I'm joking. Bank pens are always out of ink.)

Credit and Banking: (Barely) Necessary Evils

> Young men starting in life should avoid running into debt.
> There is scarcely anything that drags a person down like
> debt. . . . Debt robs a man of his self-respect, and makes him
> almost despise himself. Grunting and groaning and working for
> what he has eaten up or worn out, and now when he is called
> upon to pay up, he has nothing to show for his money; this is
> properly termed "working for a dead horse."
>
> —P. T. BARNUM, *ART OF MONEY GETTING* (1886)

There are a lot of things about the mainstream media's coverage of personal finance that annoy me. But the one that annoys me most is the incessant yammering about FICO scores.

There are three credit bureaus (Equifax, Experian, and Trans-Union), each of which produces its own FICO score (FICO is an acronym for the company then known as Fair Isaac Corporation that created the score) based on how much credit you have outstanding, how long you've had that credit, what kind of credit you have, and how good you've been about making payments on time. Scores range from 300 (Lenny Dykstra) to 850 (nobody scores that high).

The key to building a high credit score is to pay all of your bills on time and use one credit card (possibly a secured card, as we'll discuss later) very sparingly, never having more than about 20 percent of the total credit limit charged to it at any one time. So if you have a card with a credit limit of $5,000 and you have $1,000 charged to it, pay off that $1,000 before you charge anything else. This is especially easy in these days of online bill payments. Do that and only that for a while and your credit score will be good enough. Going even lower is better. Charging less than 10 percent is fantastic but, and this is where it gets tricky, if you don't use credit at all, it can hurt your score. But carrying a balance from month to month does not help your score, so please, pay off the card in full every month.

An ad I recently saw for a credit-repair company proclaimed that "Your credit score is the most important number in your life."

Really? More important than your net worth? More important than your cholesterol or body mass index?

Look, I'm not saying that FICO scores are completely unimportant, but according to Liz Weston, author of *Your Credit Score, Your Money & What's at Stake*, "There's no benefit to having scores over 800. Lenders typically reserve their best rates and terms for anyone with scores that exceed lower benchmarks, such as 740 or 760. Her advice? "Grow older. A longer credit history is a better credit history in FICO's eyes."

That's pretty much all you need to know about FICO scores. There are entire books written on FICO scores, with titles like *Perfect Credit: 7 Steps to a Great Credit Rating, The Road to 850: Proven Strategies for Increasing Your Credit Score,* and the ominously titled *Do You Make These 38 Mistakes with Your Credit?* If you find yourself with an urge to read any of these books, please have your hormone levels checked.

But some people get obsessed with FICO scores. In 2010, *Money* ran a cover story on "The Quest for the Perfect Credit Score."[2] The lead may have been the most melodramatic in the history of financial journalism: "A major league pitcher dreams of throwing a perfect game. High schoolers eyeing the Ivy League study furiously in hopes of earning 2400 on the SAT. Meanwhile, Chris Peplinski is pursuing his own brand of flawlessness: an 850 credit score."

The piece went on to profile Mr. Peplinski, a thirty-seven-year-old stay-at-home dad from Rogers, Arkansas, who "won't be satisfied until he hits the maximum: 850." According to *Money*, "To reach his goal, Peplinski voraciously reads up on every element that goes into a FICO score, checks his number every three months, and tweaks his behavior to eke out every possible additional point. Two years ago, he took out a car loan even though he and his wife, Chrissy, had the cash to buy their wheels outright. He figured that adding to his mix of credit might boost his score."

That's right: He went into debt just for the heck of it for the sole purpose of trying to boost his credit score beyond the point where there is any practical benefit. If *you* find yourself absolutely fixated on the goal of getting the highest FICO score possible, here are some tips to help you snap out of it:

- **Get a job.** A thirty-seven-year-old who stays at home with the kids and fixates on attaining a perfect credit score? Maybe, just maybe, it's time for Daddy to head back into the workforce.
- **Get a hobby.** Knitting, crocheting, making wallets out of duct tape; these are all more fulfilling activities than trying to get your FICO score as high as possible.
- **Get a shrink.** If you tell your psychiatrist that getting a perfect credit score is a major goal in your life, he or she will very likely write you a prescription for a hockey-puck-size dosage of Xanax. Even if you don't think you have a problem and don't want to use the drugs, you can very likely sell them at your local junior high school for enough to pay for a decade's worth of online credit monitoring.

The whole point of having a decent credit score is that lenders can use it to determine your eligibility for loans and the interest rates you'll pay. If you're not in the market for credit—and my goal for you is that you limit your future borrowing to the mortgage on your home that you will one day own—then you don't need to worry about it much. To a much lesser extent, credit scores can also determine how much you pay for car insurance and whether you'll be able to get an apartment lease. As we'll discuss in a second, these are not important reasons to worry about your FICO score.

Your credit score is not a measure of the strength of your financial life because your credit score does not take into account your income or your net worth. That's why it cracks me up when people say, "Your FICO score is a measure of the strength of your financial position." How could something that doesn't include how much money you make or how much money you have possibly be a measure of your financial strength?

Good Things You Can Do with a High FICO Score

1. Borrow money to buy a house with a fixed-rate mortgage
2. Use preapproved credit cards you get in the mail to scrape ice off your windshield
3. Get a slightly lower rate on car insurance, unless you live in one of the increasing number of states that prohibit underwriters from using a credit score to determine car insurance rates
4. Jimmy the lock and break back into your house if you lock yourself out

Bad Things You Can Do with a High FICO Score

1. Get a car loan
2. Cosign for a friend's loan and then get stuck with a judgment against you when the bank repossesses the moped he insisted on buying
3. Qualify for nonfederal student loans
4. Borrow money to go on vacation
5. Absolut Vodka? Abso-freakin-lutely!
6. Take your five hundred closest friends to Applebee's and pay the bill with your credit card

I hear a lot of people ask, "What about having a high credit score and lots of available credit in case I need it for an emergency?"

That's like heading to the Department of Motor Vehicles (DMV) to renew your license while carrying a double-barreled shotgun "just in case" Charlie Sheen staggers in drunkenly brandishing a pistol. You're much more likely to get yourself in trouble by giving yourself access to huge amounts of credit than you are to encounter a legitimate need for that credit. Just ask Nicolas Cage, the actor whose massive borrowing power led him to financial ruin through a string of ill-timed real estate investments. Strive for "good enough credit" accumulated over time by paying your bills religiously and leave the world of "perfect credit" to people with personality disorders. In the long run, excellent credit is good for borrowing enough money to end up with bad credit. Focus on getting good enough credit slowly, and leave excellent credit for the people with no lives.

Don't get me wrong. Having a *bad* FICO score will have a negative impact on your life. But having a limited credit history—that is, you haven't been borrowing much money—won't hurt you. Here are some myths about having a limited credit history:

> **You will not be able to lease an apartment.** You can have trouble getting an apartment if you have a track record of defaults, late payments, and repossessions, but a limited credit history won't kill you, especially if you have enough cash for a good-size security deposit. Think about it: If this myth were true, homeless shelters would be filled with high-income earners who neglected their credit. But the homeless people I see on the street usually ask for money for food, not for a subscription to an online credit-score-building program.
>
> **Some employers check your credit report before offering jobs.** This is absolutely true. But anyone who tells you that your credit *score* matters when you're applying for jobs is

misinformed. Employers are not legally allowed to check your credit score as a condition of offering a job. They are generally allowed to pull your credit *report*—but the only way this will hurt you is if you have a track record of missed payments, defaults, and repossessions. The difference between having *bad credit* and a *limited credit history* is huge, and it's something that many pundits are confused about. Having bad credit will negatively impact your life; having limited credit probably won't. No employer is going to deny you a job because you don't have a credit card. I promise.

You'll pay more for car insurance. There are many car insurers that don't even look at your credit score in determining your rate—and in some states they're not allowed to. The national average for annual car insurance premiums is $1,429[3] so we're talking about, at most, a few hundred dollars extra until you establish yourself as a good risk. Why not buy a cheap used car that you may not even have to insure for theft (who would want it?) and recoup the money that way?

The world of FICO scores is always changing—and there are some pretty strong indications that the tendency of the system to discriminate against people who don't use credit cards or car loans to build credit history will improve. Experian recently began including rent payments in the FICO scoring formula—which means that you'll be able to build a credit score by renting, negating the perceived need to borrow money in order to build a credit history.[4] There's also the FICO Expansion Score that, for a small fee, will allow you to create an alternative FICO score, called the PRBC (pay rent, build credit), that includes factors like rent payments, utilities, and cell phone bills. Log on to MicroBilt.com to find out more about that score.

The bottom line is that by requiring people to use credit cards or car loans in order to qualify for things like mortgages or possibly lower car insurance premiums, underwriters (the people who assess credit risk and make loans) are cutting out some of the smartest, safest consumers in America: people who don't believe in going into debt for things like cars, beer, and pizza. This will get fixed, maybe even by the time you read this.

Hey Fella, Why Don't You Monitor the Credit of My . . .

I was recently approached to be some kind of spokesman for a company that advertises its credit-monitoring service on national TV with catchy jingles and the promise of a free credit score. As it turned out, that "free" score comes with enough strings attached that the company has been sued by several state attorneys general and was the target of a Federal Trade Commission (FTC) investigation.

Needless to say, I turned down the opportunity (as I turn down all such opportunities to ensure that any bad advice I dole out springs from a place of sincere stupidity rather than conflicted interest).

But these credit-monitoring deals are so widely advertised and I get so many questions about them that I feel the need to bring them up. Credit scores are a very strange bird in the sense that they're one of the only reasonably cheap products (less than $20) that no one on the planet seems capable of selling you without in some way lying. Just be glad that other similarly priced consumer goods (like books, T-shirts, and DVDs) aren't sold with the same level of obfuscation. Virtually every major online seller of credit scores has at one time or another been sued by the FTC or a state attorney general for misleading consumers. Here are the facts you need to know so you don't get duped:

You can get your credit report online once a year, free, from each credit bureau. Equifax, Experian, and TransUnion. Just log on to AnnualCreditReport.com or call 1-877-322-8228 (phones? Who does that?). Get in the habit of doing this every year.

You cannot get your credit score for free. People get insanely mad about this and it is kind of BS, but whatever. If you want to know your credit score, pull out your debit card and blow a few bucks to find your score at MyFico.com or Experian .com. The 2010 Dodd-Frank financial reform bill requires companies to provide consumers with a copy of their credit score in the event that they apply for a car loan or credit card and are denied. But since you're not going to be applying for a car loan and you probably won't be applying for a credit card, this probably doesn't help you. If you have a limited credit history, you *could* go online and apply for a credit card that you know you won't qualify for—like the $300,000 credit limit Citi Chairman Card or any other card listed on CreditCards.com that requires an "excellent credit history." Once you get rejected, you can get your free credit score. But honestly, that is probably more trouble than it's worth.

If you don't want to shell out cash but are still curious about your score, log onto CreditKarma.com, where you can get a reasonably good approximation of your credit—even if not your score.

Credit monitoring is stupid. Most credit-monitoring services like MyFico.com and Experian.com cost anywhere from $10 to $25 per month—and for that price, they will provide updates on changes to your credit report and let you check your score. These programs aren't exactly awful, but they're probably not worthwhile for most consumers. If you want to sign up in the year leading up to taking out a mortgage to buy a house, it might not be a bad idea. But *Consumer Reports* doesn't recommend these programs, and consumer advocates have said there are better ways to spend $150 per year.[5]

Bottom line: If you have no idea what your credit score is and have never checked it, shell out a couple bucks and check it now. It's just good to know. Then continue to review your credit report for free a couple times per year (one free annual report from Experian each June, say, another from Equifax each January), just to make sure you're on the right track and no one has stolen your identity and cosigned on a loan for Lenny Dykstra.

Pay with Cash: The One-Step Plan to Get Rich

> Boys, they can't take my refrigerator now. They'll never get my car now. I paid cash for 'em and they're mine, and I'm keepin' 'em!
>
> —PATSY CLINE

I recently saw an ad for a credit card that "forces members to pay off their balance each month."

That's a good idea, even if you're not being forced. But there's another way to pay for stuff that will allow you to avoid debt while also forcing you to be honest about what your financial resources and limitations are. It's called cash. Conventional wisdom holds that credit cards are great—as long as you pay your balance in full each month to avoid paying interest.

It's free money! Ramit Sethi of IWillTeachYouToBeRich.com, who is very smart and right about many things but with whom I vehemently disagree about this, writes that "credit cards are like a delightful gift from heaven. If you pay your bill on time, they're actually a free short-term loan. They help keep track of your spending

much more easily than cash, and they let you download your transac-
tion history for free."[6]

The idea of a free short-term loan concerns me because it suggests that people should charge expenses to credit cards when they're
not sure if they'll have the money to cover them. The other idea you
often hear is that by using a credit card and paying it off during the
grace period before any interest accrues, you can actually earn interest
by keeping the cash in a savings account.

SWEEEEEEEEEEEEET DEAL! How much can you make
doing this? Well let me run the numbers to show you how freakin'
awesome this is:

Let's say that you charge $2,000 per month to your credit card,
and pay it off every month, keeping the money in a savings account
accruing interest at a rate of 2 percent (which is almost impossible to
find as I write this). Then, at the end of the month you pay it off,
effectively allowing you to invest $2,000 for thirty days at 2 percent
annual interest.

Here's the math: $2,000 at 2 percent annual interest for thirty
days equals . . . $3.33!

So that's the benefit of using a credit card if you do it exactly
right. You get to rack up $2,000 in debt every single month for a
chance to earn $3.33 in interest. And that's if everything goes accord-
ing to plan. One forgotten payment (and by forgotten I mean Bank
of America forgot to check its mail that day) can easily wipe out years
of that $3.33 per month benefit. But there are any number of danger-
ous activities that, if you do them exactly right, aren't harmful. Fire
walking. Bullfighting. Autoerotic asphyxiation (don't google it). The
problem is that too many people won't do them exactly right. More
than half of people who have credit cards don't pay the balance in full
each month, and the average household with credit card debt owes
$15,788.[7] By contrast, the average person who doesn't have a credit
card doesn't have any credit card debt.[8]

Everyone who gets a credit card plans to use it correctly. I've never once heard someone say, "I think I'll get a credit card and then spend thirty years paying off burgers and store-brand salsa at 23 percent interest." But that's what people do—and often they're in denial about it. In 1992, a University of Maryland economist found that although Americans had a total of $182 billion in credit card debt, they *thought* that they had just $70 billion. If you're curious, that $182 billion in 1992 had risen to $852.6 billion by 2010.

But wait! What about *credit card rewards*? Those air miles that give you a free $500 plane ticket if you spend $20,000. Isn't it so cool all the free stuff you can get for $20,000?

That's just it: When you use a credit card, you spend more money than you would if you didn't.

In 2000, the awesomely named MIT economists Drazen Prelec and Duncan Simester tested the affect of credit on purchasing by conducting a silent auction for Boston Celtics tickets—one half of the participants were told they could only pay with cash and the other half were told they could only pay with a credit card.

The result?

"On average, we found that the credit card buyers bid more than twice as much as the cash buyers bid," Prelec wrote. "That's got to be crazy, right? It suggests that the psychological cost of spending a dollar on a credit card is only fifty cents."[9] Another study found that people spend even more money when they have credit cards that offer them lots of rewards points. The Federal Reserve Bank of Chicago found that people who had cash-back rewards credit cards earned an average reward of $25 per month. But their spending increased by $79 per month in order to get that reward—and their debt went up an average of $191 over the first three months of having the card.

Purdue professor of consumer sciences and retailing Richard Feinberg conducted a spending experiment asking subjects how much they would be willing to pay for certain objects. Sometimes he placed signs for MasterCard in his office, telling the subjects to ignore them because they were for a different experiment. He found that the students who were surrounded by MasterCard signs were willing to spend more money than those who weren't. And he also found that people made their decisions more quickly when surrounded by MasterCard logos.[10] I wonder whether they would have spent less if they'd been surrounded by pictures of starving people?

This is why, as much talk as there is from smart and well-intentioned financial experts who promote cards that do things like convert your reward points into individual retirement account (IRA) contributions, I just don't buy it. I recently saw a story on a personal finance site praising a rather shameless card that used your rewards dollars as a college savings account. "Let's say you spend $10,000 a year on the credit card—that's at least $100 a year saved towards college," the personal finance expert said.

That's right! And if you spend $10,000 per year on that card for ten years, you will end up with a college savings account consisting of . . . approximately enough money to pay for a semester's gym membership. And all it cost you was $100,000, plus interest. I know it sounds nuts but there are much better ways to save money than by spending money. Like . . . by *saving* it.[11]

And airline miles? According to a study conducted by the IdeaWorks Company, Delta Airlines filled just 27.1 percent of frequent flier requests; US Airways, just 25.7 percent.[12] Airline miles can be a way to get free flights but you'll do better just paying your bills with cash, saving money, and then using that money to pay for airline tickets. It's not as sexy as bragging about all the free flights you get, but just remember: Spending tens of thousands of dollars per year in exchange for a flight does not make the flight free. Delta Airlines' mascot is not the Easter Bunny.

On a weirder note, according to a study in the *Journal of Consumer Research*, people are more likely to eat unhealthily when they pay with plastic. Researchers wrote that "there is a correlation between unhealthiness and impulsiveness of food items: Unhealthy food items also tend to elicit impulsive responses. Second, cash payments are psychologically more painful than card payments, and this pain of payment can curb the impulsive responses to buy unhealthy food items."[13] A similar Binghamton University study found that people who paid with credit cards bought, on average, 40 percent more unhealthy food than people who paid with cash.[14]

Now this raises an important question: If credit cards and obesity are linked, then why aren't most people fat and broke? Oh right, they are. If you want to be rich, thin, and beautiful, stay away from credit cards. If you want to be better than other people—like your parents—you have to be willing to be different than other people.

It's true. Most rich people aren't fans of credit cards. Billionaire software mogul and Dallas Mavericks' owner Mark Cuban once wrote a blog post called "How to Get Rich." One of his first tips? "Cut up your credit cards. If you use a credit card, you don't want to be rich."

There is a multi-hundred-billion-dollar-per-year industry working to convince you to live beyond your means and pay with plastic. If you want to be a badass, pay with cash.

Another tip: Don't just pay with any cash. Bigger bills are better. One study found that people spend less money when they pay with larger bills; those twenties and fifties are so pretty that you just want to keep them around. On the other hand, it's a lot easier to toss wrinkly old singles around.[15]

Why Do People Love Credit Cards?

But oh, we do love credit cards. Did you know that if you stacked all the credit cards in the United States on top of one another, the pile would extend seventy miles into space?

I didn't know that, either. I also don't really know what to do with that piece of information. But it was in the *New York Times* so it must be fit to print.

Part of the reason most people have credit cards is that we are absolutely bombarded with them. In 2006, 9.2 billion credit card offers were sent to Americans—and, according to one estimate, 12 percent of them actually ended up in my mailbox. That works out to thirty credit card offers per person—including children. To be fair, some of those offers were also sent to people's pets, like an eight-year-old Pomeranian named Gustaf von Coleman, who lives in Wichita Falls, Texas, and received an offer for a Visa card with a $50,000 credit limit and the promise of identity theft protection.[16] Because if there's one thing I'm sick of, it's people stealing dogs' identities.

The average adult with at least one credit card now has 3.5 of them—and half of all college students have at least four. Collectively, Americans owe about $850 billion on their credit cards.[17]

Why is this bad?

If you have $10,000 in debt at an APR of 18 percent (APR stands for annual percentage rate, aka the amount you pay in interest), you'll pay $1,800 per year in interest—and that doesn't even include the money you might put toward actually trying to pay down the debt.

If you do have credit cards and want to pay them off, don't just pay them off all at once at the end of each month. This is what most people do and, in the days of mailing checks, it was really the only way to do it. But now that most people pay their credit cards online with a direct link to their checking account, you can pay off your credit cards a little at a time as often as you can. I especially love this strategy for people who are in debt and trying to dig out. Every time you pick up a bit of cash, put it in your checking account, and then log on to your credit card account and pay down the credit card before that money magically turns into a Miley Cyrus poster that's on sale at Target. Had an especially good night working as a waiter and made $150 in tips? Deposit it into your checking account and put that money toward the balance on your credit card. Another advantage to this approach is that it will keep your average balances lower, which is good for your credit score.

Some people have credit cards thinking they somehow protect their assets in the event of identity theft in a way debit cards don't. Dave Ramsey has been debunking this myth for years but it persists. He writes: "Credit cards carry a huge risk of allowing the user to incur debt. Debit cards force you to pay with money you already have. If you hold a debit card from a well-known name like Visa or MasterCard, it will have the same policy about unauthorized charges that credit cards have."[18]

This is also a good time to make a quick comment about identity theft, which many personal finance experts are downright obsessed with. Serious identity theft problems are pretty rare and, frankly, other than being careful not to leave your debit card taped to a Post-it note with your pin, Social Security number, and mother's maiden name on the floor in Walmart, there's really not a whole heck of a lot you can do to prevent it. Your best bet? Check your credit report regularly, monitor your bank accounts and credit cards for unauthorized activity, and report identity theft the second you have a suspicion.

Another thing you need to know: You can never be held liable for debt that someone accrues when he or she steals your identity to open an account. It's the lender's responsibility for not making sure it was really you. Identity theft is bad but, honestly, most people spend way, way too much time worrying about it, because it feels better to protect yourself from the bad guys than to protect yourself from your own behavior.

Store Credit Cards

Everyone offers a store credit card nowadays. In the past few days, I've been hit up for store cards by Express, T.J.Maxx, Abercrombie & Fitch—the plastic doesn't have any hot photos on it, just a logo so I wasn't interested—and Amazon.com.

In theory, these cards can be OK. The interest rates are almost always higher than what you'd get if you went to a credit union, but if you don't carry a balance—which you shouldn't—that doesn't matter. The reason people sign up for store cards is usually the discount you get on your purchase for doing so.

One problem with store cards is that they can be difficult to keep track of, and it's easy to miss the first statement when it comes in the mail with all the bogus credit card offers. Miss one and you end up with 10 percent off an Abercrombie shirt and tarnished credit.

The other problem with store credit cards is that they tend to come with very, very low credit limits. Where a traditional credit card through a bank or credit union might have a limit of $10,000, one offered by Express, Victoria's Secret, or American Eagle might have a limit as low as $200. What this means is that your credit utilization ratio will be extremely high even with just a little bit of spending. Generally, you don't want to have more than about 25 percent of your credit limit on any card used up at any one time; ideally, you want to stay below 10 percent. The fact that you pay the bill before the end of the grace period does not affect the credit utilization ratio.

The third risk is that the stores will encourage you to spend more to get the discount (that's the whole point of them anyway). And if you increase your brand loyalty in order to get a discount, you may very well end up shopping more than you'd like, or just spending a larger chunk of your money with one retailer than you really want to. (Trust me, the head-to-toe Abercrombie look is passé.) And ironically, you get charged a higher interest rate as a reward for your loyalty.

Secured Credit Cards

Secured credit cards are normally offered to people who need help rebuilding their credit. To get one, you have to put up collateral equal to the amount of the credit limit. This is to ensure that, if you don't pay, the lender is still made whole. And while your money is sitting there as collateral, it is accruing a little bit of interest for you.

CNNMoney recently ran a story on the "best credit cards" for people with bad credit. Financial expert Rachel Ramsey Cruze (who happens to be Dave Ramsey's daughter) likened this to "a list of the best beers for alcoholics." I was going to just steal that line from her and claim I thought of it—because it does sound like something I would say—but I decided I'd do the right thing. Think of secured credit cards as being like nonalcoholic beer. They look like credit cards, offer the convenience of credit cards, and can build your credit score like credit cards—but you can't dig yourself into debt with a secured card, just like nonalcoholic beer won't inspire you to start fights with really jacked guys in the bleacher seats at minor league hockey games. Get a secured card, pay it off every month, and your credit score will improve. Someday, when you buy your first house, the interest rate on your mortgage will be lower as a result of your good credit. Over time, that will save you thousands of dollars.

Unfortunately, secured cards generally charge hefty fees. Shop around and, if you're a member of a credit union, be sure to ask whether they offer secured cards. For people who want to build their credit but fear digging themselves into debt with the temptation of a big unsecured credit limit, secured cards can be a good thing—and not just as a stepping stone to unsecured cards.

CardRatings.com recommends Orchard Bank Classic Cards. Orchard reports to the major credit bureaus. But there are any number of secured cards that will do. Just look for an annual fee of less than $40 and no application fees, and you'll be on your way to building credit without running the risk of building debt.

How Having $2,000 in a Savings Account Will Change Your Life

My dad once had a job teaching carpentry at an inner-city vocational school. After a student threw a chair at him—and one of his colleagues in the carpentry department was arrested for raping someone in a wheelchair—my dad decided it was time to return to his old job as a union carpenter.

Except the union didn't have any work for him, so they gave him picket duty. Every day, he would go and stand around with signs, chanting slogans at construction sites for projects being controlled by unscrupulous contractors.

At the end of the day, he would get a check for $25—*for the day*. It's been fifteen years since then, but he still carries around the first of those $25 checks in his wallet as a reminder to never leave a job unless you have something else lined up or you have enough in savings to last through a prolonged period of unemployment or underemployment.

This is why you need an emergency fund. Otherwise, you may end up working with a rapist while people throw chairs at you.

The other thing my dad has carried around in his wallet every day (since 1986) is a Bill Buckner rookie card.

In case you're not from Boston and/or don't know much about baseball, Bill Buckner was a first baseman for the Red Sox. In game six of the 1986 World Series, the Red Sox were one out away from winning their first championship since 1918, and the decisive play was a slow groundball to Bill Buckner. The ball rolled right through his legs, and the Red Sox lost the game and then the World Series, and the legend of the Curse of the Bambino was born.

The point is this: No matter how well everything in your life seems to be going, there is a metaphorical Bill Buckner waiting around the corner, waiting to let your dreams roll through your legs and into the outfield of despair.

So there you have it; two reasons why you need an emergency fund. If you would like your very own Bill Buckner baseball card as a reminder of this, you can get one on Amazon.com for less than $1.

The general rule for an emergency fund is that it should contain three to six months of expenses.

This is a wonderful goal and something everyone should strive for—when you reach that point, you will have a level of financial invincibility few others do: stuff can be annoying and stressful, but you aren't one relatively minor hiccup away from a financial disaster. When stuff goes badly, you can get *mad* instead of *scared*. Mad is more fun than scared. I enjoy being mad. I hate being scared.

But an alarmingly high percentage of Americans don't have that cushion. In a paper published by the National Bureau of Economic Research, Annamaria Lusardi of the George Washington University School of Business, Daniel J. Schneider of Princeton University, and Peter Tufano of Harvard Business School asked respondents to a survey, "If you were to face a $2,000 unexpected expense in the next month, how would you get the funds you need?"

The results were terrifying: 24.9 percent of respondents in the United States reported being certainly able, 25.1 percent probably able, 22.2 percent probably unable, and 27.9 percent certainly unable.[19]

If you have a financial situation where you're unable to come up with $2,000 on short notice, you are just absolutely begging for stress, anxiety, and misery.

Here's why: $2,000 is enough of a cushion to absorb most of life's relatively minor financial catastrophes (basic car repairs, bail for a relatively minor felony, taking time off from a job to audition for *American Idol*, etc.).

These things are all difficult and annoying even with money in the bank, but having enough in cash to absorb minor blows will lead to a happier, less stressful life. Of course, if you lose your job, you're still going to be in trouble, but that's where unemployment insurance can come in. There is no insurance to make up for not having a couple thousand bucks in the bank.

So, if you don't have $2,000 in a savings account, please make it your number one financial priority, right now. Eat nothing but ramen and vegetable juice for a few months; sell drugs to elementary school kids. Whatever you have to do to get a $2,000 emergency fund, do it. It will make your life so much better.

And then? Keep eating those noodles. Build it up to $5,000.

It's a good idea to keep your emergency fund separate from your checking account: preferably in a savings account liquid enough that you can get at it easily in case you need it, but not so easily that it will magically morph into the second season of *Bridalplasty* on DVD. One friend keeps his emergency fund in a savings account at a different bank without electronic access—for the sole purpose of making it inconvenient to access the money.

One quick point: A lot of people go nuts trying to find a savings account with the best interest rate. The biggest nerds among us will actually shift money from account to account chasing the best interest rates. If you are doing this over sums of money in the few-thousand-dollar range, you are wasting time and energy that would be better spent doing almost anything else. Pick one savings account and then stop worrying about it.

Once you get to the point of having a larger emergency fund (six or eight months' worth of living expenses), you might check around for a better rate; the best bet for this is usually one of the online banks like SmartyPig.com, Ally.com, or EmigrantDirect.com. All of these offer similar features and their interest rates are generally about the same because they are competing with one another for deposits.

Rule Number One of Banking: Don't Use a Bank

In mid-2011, Ikenna Njoku, a twenty-eight-year-old construction worker from Auburn, Washington, showed up at his local Chase Bank to deposit a cashier's check Chase itself had sent him. The bank suspected forgery and had Mr. Njoku arrested.

The bank eventually realized its mistake, but by then the detective on the case had left for vacation. Mr. Njoku spent the weekend in jail before the bank was able to get in touch with someone to have him released.

Auburn Police Commander Dave Colglazier told King 5 News that he was not impressed with Chase's handling of the situation.

"We do have a main line that comes into our front office," he said sarcastically. "There are ways to reach someone 24/7 at a police department."[20] But instead, Chase opted to let Mr. Njoku spend the weekend in jail and deal with it on Monday. Think about this: If you bank with Chase, you're banking with a company that doesn't realize that police departments are open on weekends. Moebs $ervices reports that overdraft fees in 2009 averaged $35 for large banks and $25 for small banks. According to J. D. Power and Associates, "Small banks have consistently rated higher in overall customer satisfaction than their Wall Street counterparts."

Once out, Mr. Njoku found his car had been towed because he'd parked it at the bank prior to his arrest. The bank took several weeks to get the cashier's check back to him and, in the interim, he didn't have enough money to retrieve his car, so it was impounded and sold at auction.

And without the car he couldn't get to his job, and so he was laid off.

In other words, if you bank with Chase, you could be arrested and jailed and lose your car and your job as a result of trying to deposit a check that *they* sent you because of money *they* owed you.

True, this won't necessarily happen to you and it could happen at any bank—not just a big national bank. But I've been following this stuff for a long time and this kind of stuff *never* happens anywhere other than at big, brain-dead multinational banks.

The other problem with the big national banks is that they generally don't know (or care) enough about their customers to set them up with appropriate products. There's so much talk about online banking and how you don't need a local branch with a local banker. I don't agree, and the data backs me up. The Federal Reserve Bank of Cleveland recently reported that "low-income homebuyers who obtain their mortgages from banks with branches in their neighborhoods are less likely to default than homebuyers who use banks without a branch in the area or mortgage brokers. This effect is especially strong among borrowers with low credit scores. While the average default rate for this group was around 20 percent, the default rate of those borrowers who took their loans from a local bank was up to 4.3 percentage points lower."[21]

It's simple: Local bankers know the markets they're working in better than national chains, and you'll have a better experience.

I hate big, national banks and I don't think people should use them. The only real advantage is that they have a lot of ATMs; but you can get cash back at the grocery store and most small banks and credit unions are now part of no-fee ATM networks anyway. So go with a credit union—or a local savings bank.

MSN recently put together a customer service Hall of Shame based on a reader poll. Five of the top ten worst companies were banks; and the only other companies on the list were cell phone companies, cable companies, and AOL.[22]

Your local credit union, on the other hand, likely isn't big enough to have an outsourced call center staffed by labradoodles; you'll get to talk to actual people about your money. Imagine that!

Here are some things to look for in a bank account:

No fees. You should not have to pay a monthly maintenance fee. Many banks have these (and many credit unions don't). Often, they'll be waived if you have a couple thousand dollars in the account. If that's the best account you can find, go with it and make that account minimum your goal: no monthly fee *and* the afore-recommended emergency dough. When you have a couple thousand dollars in your checking account, you are *mighty*.

Beware overdraft protection. Almost all banks now offer overdraft protection. This means that if you go into a store and spend $5 but only have $2 in the account, the bank will lend you the $3 difference and charge you anywhere from $15 to $35 for the "convenience" of this loan, for which they will pay themselves back as soon as you deposit more money into your account. Charging people $35 for three-day $3 loans is a really, really good business to own and a really crappy business to be a customer of. Then again, if you have $193 in your account and have handed the electric company a $200 check toward your terribly delinquent account to keep the lights on and your grandmother's dialysis machine pumping, it could be worth $15 or even $35 to keep that check from bouncing. One more reason to have a cushion: you'll never find yourself accidentally overdrawn.

You don't need a celebrity endorser. TD Bank has been running ads featuring Regis and Kelly smiling and holding their ATM cards. The point, of course, is to lure consumers who will say, "Well, I need a checking account somewhere, so I might as well go with the one Regis and Kelly get paid to say is good." Until someone comes out with an option that gives me electronic access to Regis's checking account, I'm not impressed.

Online banking. If there are any banks left that lack full-service online banking, avoid them. Online banking makes it easy to set up automatic bill payments so you never get hit with late fees, makes money transfers into savings and investment accounts easy to automate (which is the key to getting them done), and may even let you "bank" by iPhone or deposit checks without physically having to go to the bank.

Free checking. Free checking is not hard to find these days, so there's really no reason to ever pay a fee for having a checking account. Often there's a minimum balance requirement— but it's probably low enough that you can qualify for it, either immediately or by building up your emergency reserve. Sometimes you'll have to forgo the right to make deposits with a teller or receive paper bank statements in order to qualify for free checking, but those things are just vestiges of a prior century anyway.

A large network of ATMs. This one isn't crucial because you can get cash back at the grocery store when you pay with a debit card. But the key advantage to using the most widely used bank (which is different from being the most popular bank—all their customers hate it and the relationship is actually sort of creepy and codependent), Bank of America, is that there is an ATM on every corner. But recently, many smaller banks and ATMs have banded together to build their own networks of ATMs where their members can make deposits and withdrawals at no cost. Before you sign up with a smaller bank, find out how many ATMs are in its network.

Local branches. Online-only banks are growing increasingly popular. By eliminating the overhead of brick-and-mortar locations, they can offer higher interest and lower fees. Using an online bank like ING Direct for savings is great, but for your primary bank where you deposit your money, you'll feel more secure going with something local. That way, if something happens to your money, *you know where they live.*

Insurance

Chances are that someone will try to sell you an insurance policy within the next seven and a half minutes.

The only reason to say yes is if you can't afford to take the risk they are offering to insure, even though, in the long run, the odds are stacked heavily in the insurer's favor. Here are my thoughts on different types of insurance:

Health insurance. This is an absolute must because, chances are, if you have a medical emergency, you won't have $50,000 lying around to pay for it. Health coverage has been one of the hottest political issues over the last few election cycles, and there has been a change that is extremely important for you to know about. If your parents have health insurance that covers their children, you can stay on their plan at no additional cost until you turn 26. *Do not fail to take advantage of this.* In the event that you don't get health care through your job and you can't be covered by your parents' plan, Medicaid may cover you. Visit http://www.cms.gov/home /medicaid.asp. If you find yourself ineligible for these subsidized programs, you have no choice but to turn to private health insurance. At a minimum, find a program that provides insurance with high-deductible catastrophic coverage. With this type of plan, you'll still have to pay out of pocket for everyday care, but it will cover you in the event you have enormous medical expenses. A great site to visit with links and resources on this is http://www.ehealthinsurance.com /low-cost-health-insurance.

Another quick note: You can save a ton of money on eyeglasses by getting a prescription from your optometrist and ordering the glasses themselves from a site like Zenni-Optical.com, where you can get prescription glasses for $7 a pair.

Car insurance. If you have a car, you're required by law to have liability insurance. If you finance the car (which you shouldn't), you'll likely be required to buy collision and theft coverage as well. Your age, driving record, choice of vehicle, sometimes your FICO score, and even your occupation can affect your car insurance rate.

For instance, lawyers and high-level executives generally pay very high insurance rates because their jobs are viewed as stressful, and they're more likely to talk on their cell phones while driving. Scientists pay lower rates because they're seen as being very detail oriented and careful. A business owner will pay, on average, about 61 percent more for car insurance than a scientist.[23] It might not seem fair, but it's all about risk: The riskier you appear to be to the insurer, the more you'll pay for insurance. And a guy who's driving down Main Street while trying to calculate payroll taxes in his head is not the safest driver.

You can't affect your age and probably shouldn't choose your occupation to lower your insurance rate, but you sure can affect your driving record. According to Insurance.com, drivers with no violations pay on average $1,119 per year, whereas drivers with three violations pay an average of $1,713. So don't drive like a jerk.[24] Accidents, if you're in them, regardless of fault, can jack up your rates even worse than traffic violations, so drive defensively—because other people drive like jerks.

The kind of car you drive also impacts your premium. "The least expensive vehicles are ones you have to drive and no one wants to," said Kim Hazelbaker, senior vice president of the Highway Loss Data Institute, a division of the Insurance Institute for Highway Safety, in an interview with Insure.com. "The most expensive list includes cars that people don't have to drive but want to."[25] Porsches are really expensive to insure. Saturns? Not so much. A huge factor in determining insurance rates for cars is the profile of the average driver of that car. Avoid cars whose average driver is a whiskey-swigging sociopath. Do a Google image search for "Mel Gibson's Car." Then don't buy a car like that.

My advice is to buy a cheap used car no one will want to steal (no need to buy theft coverage, and it will be cheap if you do) and that you could replace if you got in a wreck.

The Internet has made it easy to find the lowest rate possible on car insurance. GEICO, Insurance.com, and other websites let you submit your information and compare quotes quickly and easily from the comfort of your home while you watch *Mean Girls* in your underwear—or so someone once told me.

Life insurance. Unless you have dependents—a spouse, low-income parents who depend on you for financial support, or a love child with your housekeeper you didn't tell your wife about for ten years—there is no reason to have life insurance. If you do need life insurance, check with a credit union, GEICO, or USAA if you're a member. No matter what, stay far, far away from "cash value" or "whole-life insurance" policies, and stick with "term" insurance. Basically, whole-life policies have a savings component to them; your premiums will be much higher each month. The fees are high, the returns are low, and you're much better off taking out the cheapest "annual renewable term" policy you can find and investing the difference in a no-load index mutual fund.

Kidnap and ransom insurance. If you're working in an area or profession that puts you at exceptionally high risk for being kidnapped—for example, gay nightclub promoter in Somalia—you or your employer may want to buy kidnap and ransom insurance. In exchange for pretty significant monthly premiums, the insurance company will pay your ransom in the event you are held hostage. This is very important because over the past six years, there has been a

100 percent increase in kidnappings. At least, that's what some website that was trying to sell kidnap and ransom insurance told me. Buy this only if your father is a disliked billionaire. But in that case, make him buy it.

Long-term disability insurance. According to the U.S. Social Security Administration, the average twenty-five-year-old worker has a 30 percent chance of being disabled for an extended period of time before retirement. Check with your employer to see whether they provide this coverage. If not, this is the one kind of optional insurance that I recommend. Check with a credit union or visit GEICO.com or ZanderIns.com.

Manufacturers' warranties on electronics. These are a complete rip-off. The only reason to buy them is if you're buying an expensive piece of equipment that is vital to your life and would present a major problem if you had to replace it. If you need a $7,000 laptop for your career as a freelance graphic designer, that's a major investment and probably worth insuring. But the $1 insurance policy Walmart tried to sell me when I bought a CD? Worthless! Plus, most products come with an "implied warranty." You can google this term to find out more, but basically it means that products have to work for the length of time a reasonable person would expect them to. So, if you buy a $200 watch and it stops working after a week, you are probably entitled to a refund even if there is no warranty.

Extended car warranties. More on cars later, but if you need an extended warranty, it's a sign you're spending too much on the car. Don't buy the extended warranty; buy a cheaper car.

Renter's insurance. Your landlord's insurance covers his or her building and fixtures. But you can buy your own policy on the value of your personal possessions and to protect you from personal liability in case of an accident. To give you an idea of the cost, I priced a policy with GEICO that would insure $10,000 in personal property along with $50,000 in liability coverage: $176 per year. The liability coverage isn't particularly valuable in terms of injuries on the property—your landlord's policy covers most of that (though not your poisoning guests with tainted vichyssoise)—but it also protects you against personal liability off the property, too (except car accidents). So, if you gouge someone's eye out doing the Soulja Boy dance at a nightclub and he sues you, the insurance would kick in.

Wedding insurance. Policies can cost as little as $150, and will reimburse you for expenses in the event of natural disasters, illness, or other reasons you have to postpone or cancel the wedding. Most of these policies won't cover you if you are stranded at the altar; those that do cover this cost way more and aren't worth it: Who would leave *you* at the altar? If you're that concerned about your fiancé or fiancée ditching you, maybe you should rethink the relationship. Check out sites like WedSure.com and WedSafe.com to learn more.

Everything else. A simple rule applies: Insure against the risks you can't afford to take; save money by "self-insuring" the ones you can afford to take. Sometimes you'll have to pay out of pocket for a new electronic foot massager, but overall, you will come out far ahead.

A word about deductibles. A deductible is the amount of money you will have to pay before your insurance kicks in. So if you have a $1,000 deductible on a homeowner's insurance policy and a $10,000 claim, your insurer will pay $9,000. One fantastic way to save money on insurance is to opt for the highest deductible you can reasonably afford;

over the long run, the saving in premiums will more than compensate for the extra out-of-pocket costs. Especially because you'll also save the hassle of making small claims— and the higher premiums often charged to people who do make claims. (Insurers like people who don't.)

The best route for most minor insurance is this: Rip *yourself* off by selling yourself insurance. Set up a savings account where you put some money in each month to cover the occasional small loss or repair.

Taxes

> If you make any money, the government shoves you in the creek once a year with it in your pockets, and all that don't get wet you can keep.
>
> —WILL ROGERS

There has never been a better time to file a tax return.

If you look at older personal finance books, they are loaded with information on how to fill out a tax return. Pages and pages and pages of tips like: "To amortize the straight-line subordinated units, factor your DOB, multiply it by your ETA, and add the GDP to your HMV minus your STD to the DMV, where applicable, between line 12, under penalty of perjury, over the top, Roger."

Today, it's different. Thank God.

Tax software is amazing. You get all your paperwork together, and then it walks you through the tax forms with a series of questions. There's no math and no fuss and, if you have a simple tax return, it's easy. The software will help you decide whether it's better to file single, single file, double-jointed, or single file jointly. Where's my joint? I'm single.

Most personal finance guides will now give you lists and lists of tax deductions and tips on how to fill out a tax return, but I'm telling you—just use the software. If you really feel like reading about the tax code, pick up the latest edition of *J.K. Lasser's Your Income Tax.*

Because of how far tax software has come—and given that you can e-file for free if your income is under $58,000 per year—most people should do their taxes at home, on their own, without an accountant. Alternatively, if your income is below $50,000 or so, the Volunteer Income Tax Assistance Program will help you for free. Call 1-800-906-9887 to find assistance in your area. But please: Always file your taxes and always file your taxes on time. Even if you owe money and don't have it, it will work out much better if you file and pay later. Remember: You can go to jail for not filing a tax return or for lying on a tax return, but you can't go to jail for not having enough money to pay your taxes.

Just Say No to Refund Anticipation Loans

One of the best reasons to file your taxes online is that you'll deprive the skeezy tax-prep people of the opportunity to try to sell you a "tax refund anticipation loan (RAL)."

For the uninitiated, these are among the biggest scams in personal finance. Here's how it works: You go into Jackson Hewitt, H&R Block, Liberty Tax Service, or any of the other tax-prep shingles that have people with limited knowledge waiting to prepare your return for a relatively modest fee (though it's still a rip-off). But what these outfits really hope to do is make you a loan against your tax refund.

Gary Rivlin, author of the fantastic *Broke, USA: From Pawnshops to Poverty, Inc.—How the Working Poor Became Big Business,* reported in *Mother Jones* that "customers wanting a RAL [refund anticipation loan] paid Jackson Hewitt a $24 application fee, a $25 processing fee, and a $2 electronic-filing fee, plus 4 percent of the loan amount. On a $2,000 refund, that meant $131 in charges—equivalent to an annual interest rate of about 170 percent—not to mention the few hundred bucks you might spend for tax preparation."

"Essentially, they're charging people triple-digit interest rates to borrow their own money," Chi Chi Wu, a staff attorney at the National Consumer Law Center, told Rivlin.[26]

Please, please, please, never take out a refund anticipation loan. Most tax preparers put the hard sell on you to try to get you to use the loans—because that's where they make their money. That's another reason to consider doing your taxes yourself using TurboTax or H&R Block's online service or a similar competitor.

Be Wary of People Telling You Things Are "TAX DEDUCTIBLE!!!"

When you file your taxes, you have two choices: itemize your deductions (things like interest payments on a mortgage and charitable contributions) or, as most people do, because for most people it's a larger amount, simply take the standard deduction—$5,800 in 2011 if you're single. (Why on earth would you take, say, $3,951 in itemized deductions, and go through all that work, when you can lower your taxable income by $5,800 with no work at all?)

What this means is that, for many people, the fact that something is deductible—like this book, but only to the extent that your investment expenses exceed 10 percent of your adjusted gross income, and then only to the extent that amount, added to your other deductions, exceeds $5,800—has no relevance. They'll be taking the standard deduction anyway.

Never spend money to get a tax deduction. Sure, if you're someone who might have enough deductions to itemize, you should include this in your calculations when you're making a financial decision. But you have to do it in a rational way—not out of a determination to pay less in taxes. The less you spend, the more you'll have.

Flexible Spending Accounts and Health Savings Accounts

One tax-saver that people ask me about is the flexible spending account, a plan that some employers offer that lets you put aside "pretax" money in order to cover health care expenses that your insurance doesn't.

The catch is that any money you haven't spent on health care at the end of the year is forfeited to your employer.

The *New York Times'* Ron Lieber offers his take on these accounts: "The accounts are a hassle. You take money out of your paycheck once to finance the account. Then you reach into your wallet for the health care expenses themselves, effectively fronting the money for a second time. Finally, you gather all your receipts and send them in for reimbursement. While there are now debit cards that allow you to pay for expenses directly from the spending account, not every practitioner accepts them. And the card companies often demand receipts anyway to prove you bought aspirin and not candy at the drugstore."[27]

Not worth the aggravation.

Health savings accounts are a better option if you have a qualified high-deductible health plan. Check with your insurer to see whether you qualify for this. It's sort of like an IRA for health care expenses.

Donate Money to the Federal Government

I mention this not because I actually expect anyone to do it, but because I think it's funny that it's actually an option.

You can donate money to the federal government for the specific purpose of paying down the national debt. It's tax deductible and, as of 2010, you can use your credit card to do it. Take a quick second to contemplate the irony of running up your credit card to pay down the national debt. It's kind of like working as a hit man and then donating the money you make to the Center for Anti-Violence Education.[28] In 2009, Americans donated a total of $3 million to the federal government for this purpose. That was enough to pay off around one quarter of one millionth of the national debt.

CHAPTER 3

The Debtonator

Debt's terrible and the sooner it's out of your life, the sooner you'll sleep better.

Student Loan Debt

I hate student loans.

In fact, I hate student loans so much that I wrote an entire book about how horrible they are, why they must be avoided, and how they *can* be avoided.

Unfortunately, not every single person who enrolled in college read it. Otherwise, I wouldn't have had to write this chapter—partly because readers wouldn't need it, but mostly because I would be living in some tropical tax haven sipping my fourth Bloody Mary at 11:00 A.M. on a Tuesday.

Anyway . . . two-thirds of graduates leave college with an average of $24,000 in student loan debt—wait, now it's $26,000 . . . $30,000 . . . wait for it, wait for it . . . $31,000. . . . Forget it. I'm not even going to try to tell you how much the average student debt load is because by the time I finish typing this sentence, it'll be higher.

But what's done is done: If you're like most people reading this book, you have student loans, and now you have to figure out how to deal with them.

First, a complaint: It's become sort of chic to tell people "You can still live your life and have a lot of fun while you get out of debt!" The CliffsNotes guide to getting out of student loan debt promises its readers that they can pay off their student loans and, at the same time, "still enjoy most of your guilty pleasures."

That's true, if your goal is to get out of debt at the age of fifty.

Here's the deal: Every single person who has made short-term sacrifices to get out of debt sooner is glad he or she did it.

Having a bunch of student loan debt is stressful—even if you don't fully realize it at the time. The happiness of being debt-free is equal to or greater than the happiness that would come from the guilty pleasures, with the added benefit that *your debt will be paid off.* Putting $1,000 toward your student loans will generate a happiness boost greater, and certainly longer lasting, than the pleasure that would come from spending it on a vacation. Just trust me on this. Please. It's so important.

It's much better to hunker down, get the debt out of your life, and then move on. The low-grade misery of chipping away at it forever is just not a good deal.

The People Who Say "Don't Pay Off Your Student Loans" Are Full of Crap

Before we get into the details of the different types of student loans and their different repayment options, let me just say that the people who tell you "Don't be in a rush to pay off your student loans" are full of crap. Financial journalists are constantly telling young people not to rush to pay off their student loans for a few main reasons. Here they are:

> **Student loans have low interest rates!** Not anymore. Unsub-
> sidized federal Stafford loans have an interest rate of 6.8 per-
> cent. That's much higher than current mortgage rates and

about six times the interest rate you can get in a savings account. Paying off your student loans and getting a guaranteed tax-free return of 6.8 percent is something you should do *before* you do anything else.

Yes, private student loans may have lower interest rates—for now—but rising rates could send your payments into the stratosphere, as I'll discuss in a little bit.

Student loan interest is tax deductible! The thing about tax deductions is that you have to lose a lot of money (the interest you're paying) in order to save a little bit of money (the value of the tax deduction). What's more, only $2,500 in student loan interest is deductible even if you paid more. And if your income is more than $75,000 per year, *none* of it is deductible. So the people who borrow big to earn a lot of money (MBAs, doctors, some lawyers) often get no tax deduction at all.

If you use income-based repayment, some of your debt will be forgiven! A couple of years ago, Congress passed a law allowing for income-based repayment (IBR), which means, if you choose, you can cap your federal loan payments at a percentage of your discretionary income. If you make income-based payments for twenty-five years (ten years if you're working in "public service," although both of these numbers may have changed by the time you read this), whatever you haven't paid off is forgiven. For most borrowers, though, there won't be any forgiveness because you will have paid off the loan in full by then, and the smaller payments you make in the beginning will cause interest to accrue and increase the total amount you'll have to pay back. Bottom line? IBR is great if you literally can't afford to make the payments on a standard payment plan; under that circumstance, IBR can prevent you from defaulting. If you can possibly avoid using IBR, using a standard repayment plan will likely save you money in the long run.

My advice is simple: Pay off your student loans. There's no "secret" to getting out of student loan debt, and if you look for shortcuts, you're likely to pay dearly.

Pay Off Private Loans First

There are basically two kinds of student loans: federal loans and private loans. You probably already know which kind you have but, if you don't, check any paperwork you've gotten and it should tell you. One hint: Stafford loans and Perkins loans are federal.

If you have private student loans, these are a potential disaster and you should pay them off first.

Almost all private student loans have variable interest rates, which means monthly payments can skyrocket with no warning and no time to figure out how you're going to pay them back.

How can you possibly feel comfortable with a loan under these circumstances? I'm not saying you should cry and lose sleep over private, variable-rate student loans you may have (although if that helps inspire you to do something about them, start bawling). But you want to get these out of your life as soon as you possibly can. As I write this, interest rates are at historic lows. Sallie Mae recently said in a press release that "Sallie Mae's Smart Option Student Loan also offers new, lower variable rates and no disbursement fees. For the upcoming academic year, rates range between 2.25 percent APR and 9.37 percent APR for degree-seeking students, based on today's LIBOR index."

You may be wondering: What is the LIBOR, why does it impact my interest rate, and what will it be in five years? Good question. The answers, in order: LIBOR stands for the London Interbank Offered Rate, it's the rate at which banks lend money to one another, and who knows?

When Sallie Mae issued that press release, the LIBOR was at around 0.75 percent. But as recently as 2007, the LIBOR was at 5.4414 percent. This means that if you had a private student loan of $50,000 based on the LIBOR + 2 percent, your interest rate would rise from 2.75 to 7.44 percent. With a $50,000 loan and a twenty-year repayment term, that means your monthly payment would jump from $271.08 to $400.96. And it is very likely that interest rates will rise from the historic lows they're at as I write this—they may even have risen by the time you read this. If there is some kind of financial crisis, or when inflation comes roaring back, as it may, the LIBOR could rise much, much higher. There is virtually no limit to how high these seemingly relatively affordable $271.08 per month payments could become.

What this means is that you want to get rid of these things *pronto*.

Please take a moment to change your underwear; we will now discuss federal loans.

Paying Off Federal Loans

When it comes to federal loans, choose the shortest repayment term you can afford. (You can switch terms later if you need to or are able to afford higher payments.) You'll have a few options.

The best option is standard repayment. This is where you make payments for ten years and after ten years the debt's completely gone. This is the best option. You'll pay the least interest and be out of debt quickly.

I know someone who's reading this is thinking, "Well, wait a second! I'll just go with the twenty-year repayment plan to give myself flexibility, but I can still pay it off in ten."

That's like saying, "I'm going to fill every cabinet in my house with Twinkies just in case there's an emergency where that's the only food that's edible, but I'm actually only going to eat raw carrots and beet juice."

We both know how that scenario ends: FAT.

So if you can possibly afford it, stick with the ten-year plan. If you need to switch to extend it later, you can. But set your sights high and see whether you can rise to the occasion.

One important question a lot of recent grads ask is whether they should save for retirement or pay off their student loans quicker. Paying off your student loan provides a nice guaranteed return. But saving in a 401(k) may get you free money from your boss! If that's the case, observe the first rule of personal finance: Accept free money.

After you've contributed up to the employer match, switch to making extra payments on your student loans. But if you really want to just focus on paying down your debt, I'm OK with that, too.

Consolidation, Schmonschmallidation

Consolidation is the process by which you take all your federal loans or all your private loans and replace them with one big loan. This basically allows you to make one big payment at the weighted average interest rate instead of a bunch of little payments. It's helpful with bookkeeping and, if you pay your bills by check, it will save you some money on postage. Private loans and federal loans can't be consolidated together (actually they theoretically can be consolidated into one bigger private loan, but they never should be) and private loans generally can't be consolidated at all right now. *Loan consolidation will not save you money.* A lot of people are confused about this. They tell me they have a lot of debt but "I'm going to consolidate it." This is the equivalent of saying "I'm 150 pounds overweight but it doesn't sound as bad in kilograms." Sometimes you can get interest rate discounts for making on-time payments with your new consolidation loan. But if you earn on-time payment discounts on some of your existing loans, you might lose them when you consolidate. In either case though, Mark Kantrowitz of FinAid.org says that "less than 10 percent of borrowers succeed in obtaining the full benefit of an on-time payment discount." On the other hand, consolidation is sometimes necessary to qualify for certain repayment programs. Visit http://loanconsolidation.ed.gov to find out about consolidating your federal loans, and use the calculator at http://www.finaid.org/calculators/loanconsolidation.phtml.

Lowering Your Monthly Payments—A Last Resort

Any method for lowering your monthly payments just kicks your problem down the road—and usually adds interest. If you are desperate, there are options to consider, but they only apply to federal loans:

> **Income-based repayment.** With IBR, if your income-based payments don't cover the full interest charges, they are waived for the first three years. But then they start up again—and are added to your principal, meaning that you will then have to pay interest on the interest. So signing up for the lower payments that come with IBR will most likely cost you more money over the long run. To learn more about IBR, and to find out what it would reduce your payments to, visit IBRInfo.org for a calculator.
>
> **Deferment.** Federal student loan servicers may let you temporarily forgo payments due to economic hardship, unemployment, military deployment, enrollment in school, internship, national service, or something similar. If you have federal subsidized loans, interest will not accrue during a deferment. If you have unsubsidized loans, interest *will* accrue. Deferment is a temporary fix for a temporary situation. If your problem is chronic, you are better off with IBR because that starts the clock on potential forgiveness after many, many years.
>
> **Forbearance.** Your federal student loan servicer might be able to offer you a twelve-month period of forbearance during which you won't be required to make payments but interest will accrue and be waiting there, anxious to mess up

your life, once you start making payments again. Use forbearance only if you have exhausted every other possible means of avoiding default. If there is any furniture left in your house or you have had even a single meal in a restaurant within the past month, you should not be considering forbearance.

Student Loan Forgiveness Options

There are a number of loan forgiveness programs out there, most of which require you to work in specific careers. Here are some of them:

AmeriCorps. If you are currently unemployed and not sure what to do, this can be a good option. If you sign up and serve for twelve months, you'll receive as much as $7,400 in stipends, plus $4,725 in loan forgiveness. Not a ton of money, but better than nothing and a great résumé builder. Log on to AmeriCorps.gov for more information.

Volunteers in Service to America. This program requires 1,700 hours of service to receive that $4,725. Yes, that's only $2.77 in forgiveness per hour, but hey, it beats the sixty-five cents an hour Montana pays its prisoners and you may be doing something more rewarding than working in the mess hall.

Military College Loan Repayment Program. This is an enlistment incentive that repays 15 percent of the outstanding principle balance of the loan annually, or $1,500, whichever is greater, for each year of service. The Air National Guard offers the same deal but instead of $1,500 it's $5,000. And if you're active duty, that 15 percent rises to 33 percent. So this is a fantastic loan forgiveness option—one of the best out there—but only if you want to pursue a career in the military for purposes other than getting out of debt.

Public Service Loan Forgiveness Program. People who work in "public service" have all their federal student loans forgiven after ten years of payments, and it can be combined with IBR. What is "public service"? Basically, any job that involves working for a nonprofit, tax-exempt 501(c)(3) organization or a federal state or local government agency. This program is actually really messed up because it assumes that people who work for the government are automatically serving the public more than someone who works in the private sector. That's right: The woman who hassled me at the DMV is eligible for loan forgiveness and someone who works long hours for slave wages at a start-up trying to find the cure for cancer is not eligible for loan forgiveness. But if you do qualify, this program can help you.

Getting Out of Credit Card Debt

> The only guy that ever calls my house is Randy from Chase Visa.
>
> —MS. NORBURY IN *MEAN GIRLS*

I sometimes wish credit cards had interest rates of 1,000 percent.

I'm guessing pretty much no one would ever run up a balance if he or she knew a $1,000 purchase would cost him or her $10,000 by the end of the year.

But in a world of 0-percent-for-six-months introductory offers (I got two in the mail the day I wrote this, and promptly sent them back, unanswered, in the postage-paid envelopes provided. Take that, Bank of America and Chase!) and low-interest balance transfers, it's all too easy to get into credit card debt.

Then you wake up one day and realize you've dug yourself into a ditch. It isn't so much the interest on credit cards that makes them lousy—although that certainly doesn't help. Really, it's the fact that it allows people to dig holes and sign off on their future earnings.

The big, dumb debate is over the order in which people should pay off their credit cards. There are even online programs that purport to help you figure this out. There are basically two schools of thought on what order to pay off credit card debt.

Suze Orman says to start by paying off the card with the highest interest rate, while making the minimum payments on the other cards (to avoid defaulting), and then, once that one is paid off, move on to the card with the second-highest interest rate.

Mathematically, that's the best way to do it and if I had credit card debt, that's what I would do. But Dave Ramsey suggests starting with the card with the lowest balance, paying that off, and then moving onto the card with the second-lowest balance—all the while making minimum payments on the rest. His reasoning is psychological. The victory of paying off one card completely will inspire you to keep at it and that, in the long run, is worth more than the interest you're saving and, by paying off each card in full as quickly as possible, you're less likely to miss payments and run into late fees.

It doesn't really matter, as long as you're paying down your debt. Just. Pay. Off. Your. Freakin'. Credit card bills.

Other things that might help:

Balance transfers. Say you owe $5,000 on a credit card at 18 percent so you transfer it to another card with a rate of 6 percent (though you might have to pay a 5 percent fee in the process). On a $5,000 balance, assuming you make no payments toward the principal, this little game will save you $350 in the first year, minus however many brain cells you burn doing this. If you have so much debt at such a high rate that you can't possibly pay it off quickly, balance transfers are worth doing. Generally though, I'd rather see you focus on paying off your debt by cutting expenses, and just getting really mad about how badly you're getting raped instead of trying to make the rape slightly less violent. Perhaps the usurious interest rate will motivate you to get out of debt faster. **Negotiating for a lower interest rate.** This is one of my all-time favorite useless personal finance tips. Self-proclaimed personal finance expert Scott Gamm advises readers to "call up your lender and ask it to lower your interest rate. Usually, lenders will lower callers' rates by 2 percent to 3 percent."[1] Sound too good to be true? It is. In some cases, lenders will reduce credit limits when people call to ask for lower interest rates—figuring the borrower is experiencing financial difficulties and is now a bigger risk. Then again, if you're about to transfer your balance to a lower-rate card, you might want to give it a try: Your current card might decide to make it attractive for you to stay and save you the trouble. **Debt management plans.** If you have a lot of high-interest debt on one card, a debt management plan can be a fantastic approach. Basically, the credit card issuer will shut down your ability to rack up new debt on the card and offer you a lower interest rate in exchange for a commitment to make payments. Call your credit card issuer's customer service line to find out whether you qualify. One quick tip: Talking with a credit card company's customer service center is among the most stressful situations anyone will ever encounter, and it is certainly not something that should be attempted sober. **Third-party debt settlement.** Just say no to any for-profit companies claiming they can negotiate a lower interest rate for you if you stop paying your cards and send them the money instead. At best these are a rip-off; at worst they're a complete scam. These companies aren't capable of doing anything you can't do, and working with one of them just might tick off your credit card company enough to inspire them to sue you for your unpaid debt. If anyone on television ever asks you to call them about anything, don't. Following this advice could have helped America avoid the tragic parts of our national history known as the ThighMaster, the Ginsu Knife, and the Ab Lounge.

Debt collection. Once your debt has been handed over to a collection agency, be aware that you are dealing with a largely unregulated industry. If you're settling a debt with a third-party collector, never give him or her electronic access to your checking account and never agree to send him or her a personal check or a post-dated check. There are just too many stories about unsavory debt collectors emptying people's checking accounts. Instead, settle your debt with a cashier's check via certified mail attached to a letter stipulating that depositing the check indicates an acceptance of that amount as settlement in full. The collector will probably whine and say that an electronic funds transfer would be better, but he or she will eventually cave. One important note: If you owe $12,000 and the bank settles for $3,000, you will likely have to report that $9,000 in forgiven debt as income and pay taxes on it. So be ready for that.

Nonprofit credit counseling. In general, the best way to get out of credit card debt is to stop using all of your cards, spend less money, work as much as you can, and throw every nickel you can at your debt. But in some cases that may not be enough. If you just can't seem to make headway, visit the National Foundation for Credit Counseling's website at http://www.nfcc.org, and find a counselor in your area. She or he will go over your finances with you, offer solutions, and perhaps set you up with a debt management plan.

Bankruptcy. The last resort. Financial expert Dave Ramsey, who filed for bankruptcy himself in his twenties before turning his financial life around, calls it a "gut-wrenching, life-changing event that causes lifelong damage. . . .

Bankruptcy is listed in the top five life-altering negative events that we can go through, along with divorce, severe illness, disability, and loss of a loved one."[2] It drives me nuts when so-called financial experts recommend bankruptcy like it's some sort of pedestrian solution to problems. If you do decide to talk to a lawyer about bankruptcy, be extremely careful. Many run bankruptcy mills, where he or she files for anyone who walks into his or her office and collects the fee. You need to find a lawyer who's part lawyer, part therapist, and will look at all the options with you to decide whether bankruptcy really does make sense for you. I don't judge people who do have to file for bankruptcy, and certainly there are situations where it's unavoidable, but it's not something ever to rush into. Do everything you can to avoid it.

CHAPTER 4

Fahrenheit 401(k)

October. This is one of the peculiarly dangerous months to speculate in stocks. The others are July, January, September, April, November, May, March, June, December, August, and February.

—MARK TWAIN

Now that we've gone over all the ways you can get ripped off by the banking industry, I want to teach you how you can get ripped off on the investment side. Isn't this fun?

But first, we must remember the number one rule of investing, and it's one that, unfortunately, many of my competitors' personal finance books don't even mention. *Do not invest all of your money in stuffed animals.* I recently interviewed a retired soap opera star who lost his kids' six-figure college funds on Beanie Babies. Bad! At most, 25 percent of your portfolio should be in stuffed animals. (Or, lest I mislead the sarcasm-impaired, let me be clear: by "25 percent" I mean "none.")

Beanie Babies aside, there are plenty of other ways you can get ripped off when figuring out where to invest your money, but it doesn't have to be that way. Finance is one of those fields where, if you do a few things right, everything else is just drama. If you save and invest regularly, starting as early as you possibly can—and you stay away from debt—you will have a wonderful financial life.

To do this, take a page from the playbook of the IRS, which—no matter how you feel about it—is about as good at getting what it wants as any organization in the world.

In 1943, the U.S. government was concerned that it wasn't collecting as much in taxes as it should. The gap between the income tax that should have been collected and the amount that was collected was troublingly large, and it seemed people were earning enough money but then spending it, so when the time came for them to pay taxes, well golly gee, they just didn't have the money. So the IRS implemented what is now known as the withholding tax by which the government intercepts a chunk of each paycheck that workers receive before it gets into their bank account. If you've ever looked at your first check from a job and shouted "WHAT THE #$%#! IS FICA AND HOW DID IT GRAB MY MONEY?!?!?" the answer is the withholding tax.

The feds did this because they knew that if the government didn't get paid first it wouldn't get paid at all. The program has been a tremendous success in terms of generating revenue.

It's also a model that's easy enough to apply to your own life: Before you pay any other bills, make sure that a chunk of change from your income is diverted toward saving and investing. Pay yourself first.

According to the 2006 U.S. Census, the median income for someone over the age of twenty-five with a bachelor's degree was $49,303.

If you divert 10 percent of that amount into your 401(k), you'll be saving $4,930.30 per year (and lowering your taxes, too). If you save $4,930.30 per year starting at age twenty-five and invest it for an average annual return of 10 percent (hard to do, but fun for illustration— and actually about in line with the average annual return in the stock market over the long term), you will have $2,623,467.19 by the time you're sixty-five. If you have an employer match, you could end up with 50 percent more, or even 100 percent more, depending on how the match works. The two most common approaches seem to be a match of 50 percent up to the first 6 percent of your salary (so if you earned $50,000 and contributed $3,000, your employer would toss in another $1,500) or 100 percent up to the first 5 percent—which is much better. You get paid $50,000, you put in $2,500, and your employer kicks in another $2,500. One of the few rules of money is: Don't turn it down when it's free. You must *always* contribute to your 401(k) up to the maximum employer match.

If you wait until you are thirty-five, in this example you'd end up with just $978,136.16—a difference of more than $1.6 million, even though you saved only $25,000 less.

If you wait until you are forty-five to start doing this, you'd end up with just $343,789.82.

If you had a decent math teacher in high school, you probably already understand how this works. But perhaps you didn't have a decent math teacher, or perhaps you weren't paying attention. Or perhaps, like me, you weren't in class that day because you got kicked out for passing a bottle of scented hand sanitizer to a friend (true story). Basically, the gains from compound interest grow exponentially the farther you go. If you have $1 and invest it at 5 percent, you have $1.05 at the end of the first year; but how much do you have at the end of the second year? If you guessed $1.10, you're way off. You'd actually have $1.1025. OK, so this example isn't very impressive. But as you go further out into the equation, it starts to really add up.

Here's a real-life, approachable, everyday scenario to show you how this works. In 2008, according to PNC Wealth Management, the gifts from the song "The Twelve Days of Christmas" (four calling birds, three French hens, etc.) would have cost $86,609.[1]

But if the baby Jesus had been presented with $86,609 worth of mutual funds in the year 0 and they had compounded at an annual rate of 12 percent until the year 2011, those mutual funds would be worth . . . $9.20925793 \times 10^{103}$. This is a ton of money. In fact, it's far, far greater than the total net worth of the entire planet.

However, you might not have $86,609. As a matter of fact, Jesus did not have that kind of money, and there are no investments that have a 2,012-year history of generating returns of 12 percent.

Even if Jesus had been given only $1 on his birthday and it had compounded for 2,012 years at just 2 percent per year, he still would have ended up with $201,161,833,320,078,880. *That's not a typo*: 201 quadrillion dollars. And it can be yours, too, if you have $1 and 2,012 years. In other words, with all the economic growth, population growth, and other drama we've had since Jesus was born, he'd actually be 3.2 million times richer than Warren Buffett if he'd just been given $1 on his birthday, as long as he'd invested it at 2 percent instead of spending it on frankincense or myrrh.

There are so many problems with this hypothetical that I don't even know where to begin. Actually, it helps to illustrate why the 10 percent rate so often used to encourage stock market investing, as I used it above, is very possibly too optimistic. Or possibly not optimistic enough. Who knows what will happen over the next forty years? But if it is too optimistic, that only argues for starting *sooner*, and saving *more* to reach financial independence.

Two thousand and twelve years of compound interest will do wonders for your retirement account, and so will fifty years. You are so lucky, being younger than your parents, let alone your grandparents, because you have so much more time for the magic of compound interest to make you rich. But you have to start now and not make excuses. The people who win with money are the ones who save 10 to 15 percent of their money every year before they do anything else.

Archimedes said, "If you give me a lever and a place to stand, I can move the world." I say, "If you give me $1 and a couple thousand years, I can create 3.2 million times as much wealth as Warren Buffett without having to do anything other than open a Roth IRA."

This is the miracle of compounding. The greatest benefits from compounding come the farther into the equation you go. By giving your money more time to compound, you will end up with more money—*exponentially* more money. And the only way to give your money more time to compound is to start early.

How to Become Wealthy

It's a cliché: "It's not how much you make, it's how much you keep." But it's true! Economists Steven Venti of Dartmouth and David Wise of Harvard found that income differences account for only about 5 percent of the differences in household wealth.[2]

The way that people accumulate wealth is that they *decide* to save a significant chunk of their income. Most people of all income brackets don't do this, and that's why most people never accumulate any significant assets.

What matters in wealth building is the decision to live a life that allows you to save a significant portion of your income. There's no secret, there's no trick. Doing it is more important than how you do it. Just *do it*. This is great news because it puts your financial future in *your* hands, not your boss's or anyone else's.

You may be asking yourself, "Why should I save money for retirement now? Isn't it more fun to spend? Live in the moment!"

No. Once you get started with this plan you will find that, paradoxically, saving for retirement is actually more fun than spending on cool stuff. You'll have a feeling of power and control over your life. You'll sleep better at night knowing that you're making progress toward financial power—the ability to be true to yourself. Plus, it's extremely unlikely that your parents were saving money at your age so this move will automatically make you *smarter than the people who raised you*. Which means that—for the rest of your life—you can yawn with dismissive condescension whenever they try to give you advice.

How much do you need to save? Investment adviser Dan Solin, author of *The Smartest Investment Book You'll Ever Read*, researched this and found that, in order to enjoy a comfortable retirement—one that doesn't involve a massive plunge in standard of living—people need to save an average of 15 percent of their pretax income throughout their career.

If you make $40,000 per year, that works out to $6,000 per year. If you can live on $40,000 per year, you can live on $34,000. If you do, you will feel competent and secure—filling 40 percent of the tiers on Maslow's hierarchy of needs, and also making it easy to fill the other levels. Here are some tricks for doing this painlessly:

> **Make it automatic.** Diverting money automatically each week, biweekly payment period, or monthly from your paycheck (or bank account, in the event that you're self-employed) to a 401(k), savings account, and/or IRA is the best way to get rich because, once it gets set up, it doesn't require any willpower. Making it the default requires a conscious decision to *stop* your plan rather than a conscious decision to continue. When your default option is smart, you're more likely to stick with it. We're lazy. If the easy option is the smart option, we'll do the smart thing.
>
> **Invest your tax refund.** Every year around April, when people start filing their taxes and getting their tax refunds, nearly every personal finance guru starts admonishing people to adjust their withholding tax for the following year to keep more money in their paychecks and lower their refund. "Stop lending money to the government for free, idiot!" we're told. But studies show that we're more likely to save large amounts of money than small amounts of money, and if you get a $1,000 tax refund at the end of the year, that's a great place to start your retirement saving. Sure, you could have your employer adjust your withholding and get a slightly larger paycheck and no refund. And you could invest a few dollars each week or month from that slightly larger paycheck—but, more likely, you'd "accidentally" spend it. Having too much

tax withheld throughout the year and then investing the refund is a painless, discipline-free way to invest.

Enroll in your company's retirement plan. If you have a job that offers a 401(k), or a 403(b) if you work for a nonprofit, you absolutely must sign up for it. Talk with your boss to find out who to call to get this set up. If you make every single financial mistake in the world but contribute up to the maximum employer match on your 401(k) and never touch that money until you retire, you will end up with a vastly better financial life than most Americans. It's just that simple. If your employer offers a Roth 401(k), even better. You don't get the up-front tax deduction but you won't have to pay any taxes when you withdraw the money. By forgoing the tax deduction now to avoid any tax later, you'll be sitting even prettier when you do start withdrawing the money. (It's not that your parents were too dumb to do this; just that until recently, Roth 401(k)'s didn't exist.) If you switch jobs, you can roll over the 401(k) from your old job into a 401(k) at your new job; if you go freelance or become unemployed, you can roll the 401(k) over into an IRA. Do not, under any circumstances, ever, cash out your 401(k) when you leave a job, or for any other reason. Once the money is in the 401(k), it stays there until you are old enough to answer the question "Boxers or briefs?" with "Depends." OK? Never. Don't take a 401(k) loan, and especially don't withdraw money from your 401(k). Taxes and penalties will leave you with about fifty cents for every dollar you're taking out, and will set back your retirement plan by a *lot*. From setting up your 401(k) to changing it when you switch jobs, the human resources person at your job will be able to coordinate this for/with you. This all seems very intimidating and bureaucratic—and it is—but it's just a matter of talking with the right person at your company. Happily, many companies now enroll their employees in a 401(k) plan unless the employee specifically opts out of it. The idea is that by making the best option for you the default option, your laziness will trick you into acting in your own best interests. This is also, by the way, why automating the most important financial planning aspects of your life—retirement contributions—is so important.

Roth IRA. If your income is under $110,000 per year, you can contribute up to about $5,000 per year to either a traditional IRA or a Roth IRA. There are all kinds of calculators that can help you decide whether you should use a traditional IRA (where contributions are tax deductible but you have to pay income taxes once you withdraw the money) or a Roth IRA (where contributions are not tax deductible but you never pay any taxes on your gains). But if you're young enough to have picked up this book, go with the Roth IRA and forget I ever even mentioned traditional IRAs. Taking that $5,000 out of your bank account and putting it in the Roth IRA won't save you money on taxes today, but makes all the money you—or *your* kids—eventually withdraw from it tax-free. Given how many years of growth your money has ahead of it, the latter option is better. The other thing I love about Roth IRAs is that you can withdraw your principal (the money you put into the account) without paying any taxes or penalties. This means that if you open a Roth IRA and decide in a few years that want to use the money you have put in there to buy a house or pay for grad school, you can do so without penalty (though I would try to talk you out of it—because of how much that cash would have grown over the ensuing decades if you left it in the IRA). But the point is that with a Roth IRA, you at least have that option. It's good to have options.

SEP IRA. If you're self-employed or have freelance income, as an ever-increasing percentage of young people do, the SEP IRA is a wonderful thing. You can invest up to 25 percent of your self-employment income and lower your taxable income by that amount. The formula for the contribution limit is needlessly complicated, but an accountant or tax software will walk you through how much you can contribute.

Individual 401(k). This is a fantastic plan for people who have a full-time job but also freelance on the side. With an individual 401(k) you can put 100 percent of your first $15,000 in self-employment earnings into the 401(k), lowering your taxable income by that amount. In addition, you can contribute a percentage of your income. The paperwork and administrative crap associated with these accounts is somewhat more complicated than it is with a SEP IRA, but if you have a relatively low self-employment income, you'll be able to contribute a much greater chunk of it to an individual 401(k) than you'll be able to put in a SEP IRA. If you have a pretty high self-employment income and are able to contribute a huge chunk of it to your retirement plan, an individual 401(k) will let you contribute more money. If your income is really high, the contribution limits are the same. For details, google "SEP IRA versus Individual 401(k) calculator".

All I'm asking you to do is value your own future—and present the ability to sleep at night knowing that you have the resources to handle the butt-kicking that life hands almost everyone at some point. Can you do that?

You *think* you'll never live past forty, let alone fifty-nine and a half—the age at which you can start withdrawing retirement funds without penalty—who would want to? But ask your folks: *They* want to.

The Nitty Gritty on 401(k)s

What should you do with the money in your 401(k)? You'll be offered so many different mutual funds to choose among! To begin with, look for funds with very low expense ratios. The expense ratio is the percentage of your money the fund manager takes each year as his or her fee. A 1 percent fee may not sound like much, but in a world of 2 percent bond yields, that can be half your return! (Imagine if poor baby Jesus had had to give up half of the 2 percent we imagined his money earning for 2,012 years. Instead of $201 quadrillion, he would have had only $495 million!) The expense ratios are listed on the form that gives you the different investment options. "Index" funds, if offered, are likely to have by far the lowest expense ratios.

If your plan offers it, go with something called a "Total Stock Market Index Fund."

Many 401(k) plans, especially at smaller companies, offer *only* high-fee investment options. This is really unfortunate but the truth is that the tax breaks that come with saving in a 401(k)—and the employer match if yours offers one—far outweigh those fees. And look: Over time, you and your fellow employees may be able to shame management into offering better choices. Or, when you leave your job, you can roll the 401(k) into an IRA with Vanguard or Fidelity, and benefit from their low-cost index funds. But in the meantime, you're building a big retirement fund anyway.

Many people will look at the fund options and choose the "Balanced Fund," which seems like a good idea because it sounds prudent and actually kind of Zen. But if you're in your twenties or thirties, the Balanced Fund is too conservative because it contains something like 40 percent bonds. Over time—and being young, time is on our side—stocks do much better than bonds. There's more risk in the short run, but you're "paid" to take that risk by the likelihood of much greater gains over the long run.

It can be very tempting to be hyper-conservative because of the tremendous volatility we've seen in the stock market recently. But if you're investing for retirement in twenty-five, thirty-five, or forty-five years, you should not be worried about volatility. For us, the biggest risk is investing too conservatively and not having our money grow fast enough to outpace inflation and pay for the very, very high-tech cribbage boards we will want in our golden years.

A quick point about company stock. Your employer might offer you a chance to take shares of the company you work for as part of your 401(k). I'm OK with having a very small percentage of your 401(k) in employer stock, but in general it's a bad idea. Your financial life is already exposed enough to your company. If the company does well, you'll have job security and probably raises and promotions. Your investments should diversify your life away from your job, not make your entire life dependent on it. I'll never forget seeing the video where an Enron human resources manager advised employees to put all their 401(k) money into Enron stock. This led to disaster: their retirements were wiped out at the same time as their jobs.

A note on 401(k)s versus IRAs: If you have income low enough to qualify for a Roth IRA—as most people do—you should contribute to your 401(k) only up to the point of the maximum employer match. Put any additional savings you can muster into a Roth IRA and max that out before contributing more to your 401(k). If you want to save still more after that, you must be living in your car.

What happens if you leave your job? It means you need to roll your 401(k) over into an IRA, which is not as complicated as it sounds. Just call Vanguard or Fidelity (or T. Rowe Price, or whomever). They will walk you through the process. Easy-peasy and it's actually better than having your money in a 401(k) because you will often have lower-cost investment options.

The Nitty-Gritty on Roth IRAs

Roth IRAs are a lot easier to write about than 401(k)s because everyone who qualifies (single filers with income below $110,000, joint filers with income below $173,000; the contribution limit phases out quickly above these income levels) has the exact same options.

You can contribute up to $5,000 per year to a Roth IRA, and

then pay no taxes on its growth or, when you reach retirement age, withdrawals.

This is a good deal. To take advantage of it, I suggest you log on to Vanguard.com (or Fidelity.com—or any other broker, but Vanguard is a really wonderful company) and set up an account. I don't have any kind of endorsement deal with Vanguard but it's the company I use, and they're fantastic. Vanguard has a $3,000 account minimum for opening a Roth IRA but it's worth waiting a bit until you have that much to benefit from their superior service, prices, and general competence.

In deciding where within Vanguard to invest your account, I recommend choosing a "target date fund"—the target date is based on your current age—filled with index funds. It's not exciting and probably won't impress the coffeehouse cognoscenti but, in the long run, it will lead to results that beat the vast majority of investors.

If your income is too high to contribute to a Roth IRA (bully for you!), you can contribute to a traditional IRA. Vanguard and the others will walk you through this as well.

Investing for the Long Term

It might be hard to imagine it now, but the average long-term return from investing in the stock market has ranged somewhere between 8 and 11 percent for the past hundred years or so—enough to keep up with inflation and still make real gains, if those gains weren't eaten up by fees and taxes along the way.

During *our* young lifetime, the long-term return of the stock market has been such that you almost would have been better off spending your money on beer, drinking it, and then returning the empties. Well not quite, but it's been pretty bad and, if you'd invested in Internet stocks during the bubble, it actually would have been that bad.

We're part of a generation that probably doesn't remember the good times. During our lifetime—or the part of our lifetime where we were aware of what was going on—the stock market has been a hyper-volatile source of stress and depression. But for the long run, you have to believe in the ability of a broadly diversified portfolio of public companies to generate value for their shareholders.

Put simply: If the stock market isn't dramatically higher in fifty years than it is today, the world will be such a radically different place that your investment choices will be the least of your concerns.

And that's just the market as a whole, including all the stocks that will do badly. If you avoid those, and just buy the ones that go up (*duh!*), you'll do much better still. As Will Rogers said, "Don't gamble. Take all your savings and buy some good stock, and hold it 'til it goes up. Then sell it. If it don't go up, don't buy it."

The problem? That's really, really hard, and probably even impossible, to do.

Here's the dirty little secret of the investment world (well, it was a secret until wonderful books like *Bogle on Mutual Funds, A Random Walk Down Wall Street*, and *The Only Investment Guide You'll Ever Need* exposed it): You probably won't be able to, through superior research or intelligence, achieve superior stock market returns.

Indeed, while the market as a whole has produced 8 to 11 percent returns over time, between dividends and price appreciation (though before inflation and taxes), most people have probably realized more like 4 or 5 percent (still before accounting for inflation). How do the stock market's long-term returns get halved like that? Because people invest their money with fund managers who charge them too much—and then don't deliver the performance to justify their fees. Then, people move in and out of the market too often, triggering taxes and more fees. And, when humans try to time the market, they tend to buy high and sell low. That is, after all, how the stock market works. When the market's falling, that means a lot of people are trying to sell. When the market's soaring, it means most people are trying to buy. Most of the wealth lost in the 2008 market crash was lost because people freaked out and sold at the bottom; investors who hung on ended up seeing their portfolios rebound.

For the twenty-year period ended in 2009, the S&P 500 rose 8.2 percent annually. The average investor in a stock market mutual fund earned just 3.2 percent per year.[3] In dollar terms, that means he or she turned $10,000 into $18,775.61 over those twenty years. During that time, investing directly in the S&P 500 would have grown that $10,000 into $48,366.56.

Remember that John Bogle quote about what's good for the financial industry is bad for you? The mutual fund world is a fantastic example of this.

There is no evidence—and, in fact, there is an overwhelming amount of evidence to the contrary—that investors can beat the long-term returns of the stock market through superior stock selection or by timing the market. Famous studies have shown that randomly selected portfolios of stocks (monkeys throwing darts at a list of companies) perform just as well as the highest-paid mutual fund managers in the world. Sure, some mutual fund managers and stocks will outperform the averages. Just like some hookers don't have STDs. But because you don't know which is which, your best bet is to just buy the entire lot. OK, that analogy didn't work. The point is that earning the market's average return means earning a return that is better than most investors, and so that's what you should try to do. Not least because it's so easy.

There's an old line about a fund manager walking into the office and telling his colleagues "I have good news and I have bad news. The bad news is we just lost a ton of money. The good news is that none of it was ours." "What was the bad news again?" ask his confused colleagues.

The math of managing a mutual fund works like this:

Your fund is up 10 percent this year: Buy a new Mercedes.

Your fund is down 10 percent this year: Buy a new Mercedes.

Your fund is flat this year: Buy a new Mercedes.

This is a great business to be in, but a crappy business to be a customer of. One of the best financial books of all time is *Where Are the Customers' Yachts?* published in 1940. Not much has changed since then, except that the yachts have gotten nicer. That's the nature of the financial services industry as a whole: a few winners (driving Mercedes) and a whole bunch of losers (us).

Mutual fund fees are calculated based on assets under management—not performance. Vanguard's flagship index fund, the Total Stock Market Index Fund, has an expense ratio of 0.18 percent. This means that for every $1,000 that you have invested with them, Vanguard will charge you $1.80 in fees each year. Compare that with another fund that has an expense ratio of 2 percent—that works out to $20 each year in fees on a $1,000 investment. Remember Jesus's $201 quadrillion? All gone in fees and expenses. Blessed are the meek—and a good thing, too.

Assuming both funds return the same pre-expense performance of 10 percent annually (remember, there is no evidence that more expensive funds are able to provide better performance than less expensive funds; indeed, the very act of trying is likely to rack up extra expenses and tax exposure), your performance will look like this:

- After twenty-five years, $5,000 invested in your Vanguard Total Stock Market Index Fund will be worth $52,000.
- After twenty-five years, $5,000 invested in the fund with the 2 percent expense ratio will be worth $34,242.

The $17,758 difference is all a result of fees. It's like a diet bar that charges you five pounds around your midsection; in order for it to be a good deal—and, in fact, not detrimental to your health—it must help you lose weight by an amount greater than the amount of fat it adds to your midsection. Some actively managed mutual funds will outperform the indexes—just as, of the hundreds of thousands of

people who bet on the Kentucky Derby, some will win. But there is
no way to predict which ones. Study after study has proven that. It's
a loser's game, and the only way you can win is by not playing it, that
is, buying index funds. About 80 percent of mutual funds underper-
form the indexes over the long term. Let me say that again: About 80
percent of people who are specially trained and highly paid to perform better than the market end up performing worse than you
could by just buying all the stocks with an index fund. In any other
field, they'd be fired; in money management, they get a yacht. You
can do better than 80 percent of people who try to play this game just
by skipping the game and buying index funds.

Besides Vanguard, other low-expense index mutual funds
include Fidelity Spartan 500 Index Fund Investor Class (Fidelity
.com), Schwab S&P 500 Index Fund (Schwab.com), and CIBC U.S.
Broad Market Index Fund (CIBC.com).

If you want to do your investing through your bank or credit
union, you can talk with the investment person there and say you
want to open an account and invest exclusively in index funds—and
don't let him or her bamboozle you into anything else. Including an
index fund that charges an unnecessarily high fee. Any of these broad
market index funds provide a ton of diversification, and these funds
will all perform very similarly over the long run. There is no advantage to investing money in more than one of these funds, as it will just
leave you with more paperwork.

It is also important to make sure that your investments have
some international exposure. You don't want to go too heavy with
this because foreign markets and especially emerging ones can be
more volatile than the United States but, somewhat paradoxically, a
portfolio with just U.S. stocks is actually riskier than one that has a
mixture. Ideally, the life-cycle fund that you choose will have some
international exposure—another reason that I like Vanguard. If you
decide to add international exposure on your own, invest no more
than perhaps 30 or 40 percent of your portfolio in funds like Fidelity

Spartan International Index Fund and Vanguard MSCI Emerging Markets Fund.

Another way to accomplish the same thing: exchange traded funds (ETFs). These are equivalent to mutual funds that are like stocks. Instead of a share of Apple you buy a share of an ETF. Most ETFs are index funds and offer similarly low fees. Apart from convenience, they offer no advantages I can see over traditional index mutual funds. And the fact that they *are* so easy to trade online can induce investors into selling out of fear, or trying to trade them speculatively. Or, you might find yourself cashing in ETF shares to cover some impulse splurge and you later wonder WHAT THE HELL WAS I THINKING? Cashing out of traditional mutual funds takes a few more days; this is a good thing. Think of it as a bureaucracy-imposed cooling-off period that will actually work in your favor over the long run. There's no real advantage to being able to access your cash a few days sooner: My bookie almost always gives me five business days to come up with the cash before he punches me in the stomach

Here's what you need to know about investing: Following stock tips, hiring expensive advisers, and investing in mutual funds managed by professionals does not generate enough in increased returns to justify the costs. Instead, it drags down your returns. This is why fewer than 10 percent of mutual funds beat the market's averages over the long term—and it's impossible to predict which funds will outperform in the future because, as the fund's ads touting results warn in the fine print: *Past performance is not a guarantee of future results.*

A perfect example of this is Legg Mason Capital Management Value Trust. That fund, managed by Bill Miller, beat the S&P 500's returns for fifteen consecutive years—1991 through 2005—an unprecedented streak.

A handful of books and literally thousands of magazine and newspaper articles were written on Bill Miller's brilliance. Then in 2006, it all fell apart. From 2006 through 2008, the fund tanked, performing even worse than the stock market as a whole, which was absolutely pulverized. The performance was so bad, in fact, that investors would have been better off sticking with an index for the fund's entire existence.

If you want to get rich, you should invest like a girl. Seriously. A 2011 study conducted by Barclays Wealth and Ledbury Research found that women performed better in the market than men, and a 2009 study found that, over the long term, women earn about 1 percent more per year on their investments than men.[4] The reason? Women, with some exceptions like Nancy Grace, aren't testosterone-fueled egomaniacs who think they're brilliant and better than everyone else. Men try to be brilliant and creative; women, on average, just buy their mutual funds and sit tight. That's the approach that wins.

Some people look at studies like this and go overboard. Andrew Tong, a former trader for a New York hedge fund, filed a lawsuit against his boss after, he alleged, he was pressured to take female hormones in order to make himself a better trader. These hormones allegedly led to cross-dressing. Hey, whatever works, but I suggest just sticking with index funds.

You can't beat the market. Almost no one can. As William Bernstein, author of *The Intelligent Asset Allocator*, puts it, "There are two kinds of investors, be they large or small: Those who don't know where the market is headed, and those who don't know they don't know." The few exceptions have absolutely no interest in helping you, even if you could figure out who they are.

Instead, benefit from the lower costs and enjoy the long-term growth of the world economy.

Why I Recommend Life-Cycle Funds Over "Do It Yourself" Asset Allocation

A lot of people don't like life-cycle funds because they don't like the idea of having their money managed via algorithm—gradually growing more conservative as they age.

A personal finance blogger and I were arguing about this recently. He hates life-cycle funds and told me that he's "too much of a control freak for that." He figures he "should look at [his] stuff at least once a year, then make a wise decision."

The trouble is, you probably won't make a wise decision. If you decide to allocate your own capital once a year, you will most likely end up lowering your investment in the stock market after the market falls—and then adding to your exposure after the market goes up. Or, you'll end up selling stock because you get scared by headlines about economic uncertainty. This is a guaranteed way to end up underperforming; letting these life-cycle funds handle the whole thing for you lets you avoid that.

This is what I would call a very convenient truth: The less time you spend trying to become a great investor, the more likely you are to achieve great results. Plus, it's easier. Instead of spending your time looking over spreadsheets trying to decide whether your exposure to the Malaysian mining industry should be 0.0002 or 0.0003 percent, you can engage in more productive and fulfilling activities like, for example, *anything*.

The other common criticism of life-cycle funds is that it's hard to say which ones are the best. If you go with funds from the big index fund families like Vanguard and Fidelity, they are basically the same. The exact allocations (what percent is in stocks, what percent is in bonds, etc.) will differ slightly but probably not by enough to really make any difference. And, even if it does make some difference, you couldn't predict today which one will perform better because experts aren't in universal agreement on the specifics of exactly what percentage of your money should be invested in each asset class.

The greatest problem experts have with life-cycle funds, I believe, is that they make it easy for small investors to handle their funds themselves, and negate the need for experts. But that's a big part of why I love them!

The One-Step Guide to the Financial Media

The media has a habit of giving extremely strange financial advice—with an almost perfect track record of god-awful timing.

In 1977, for instance, this was—and I swear to God I'm not making this up—the lead in a *Boston Globe* story: "If the stagnant stock market has you baffled as to where to put those extra dollars you'd like to invest, you might consider collector's plates."

Seriously. One of the best and most respected newspapers in the country recommended "limited edition"—that is, limited to however many they could find buyers for—collector's plates as an alternative to the stock market.

I've often suspected that many people choose to go into the world of financial reporting less out of an interest in economics and more out of a profound sense of repression and sexual frustration. Otherwise, how would we end up with headlines like these:

Stock Market Gyrates from Libyan Oil Crisis[5]
Investors Pull Out on Fear Factor[6]
Bottoming Is a Messy Process[7]
Stock Market Probing Short-Term Bottom[8]
10 Reasons to Wack Obama's Stimulus Plan[9]

The moral of the story? Ignore the hype and the scare tactics, and stay the course. One study found that individuals with brain damage that impacted their ability to feel emotions actually performed better in an investment game than people with normally functioning brains.[10] So ignore the media, keep your emotions out of it and, if that doesn't work, consider an ice-pick lobotomy.

As a recovering member of the financial media, it pains me greatly to say this, but your best bet for handling advice on when to buy and when to sell is: Ignore all of it.

No one can predict which way the market is going to go in the short term, and only a fool would go on television and claim otherwise. The problem is that many fools do go on television every day with predictions about the market. Sometimes they're earnest, well-intentioned people but they're wrong half the time. In an article in the newsletter of the American Association of Individual Investors, investment strategist Dick Davis puts it this way: "I believe one of the worst things that can happen to a long-term investor is to be instantly and totally informed about his stock. In most cases, spot news fades into irrelevance over time. . . . Big market moves may be inexplicable, but a long-term . . . approach precludes the need for explanations."[11]

You and I are simply far too young to sit around worrying about month to month—or even year to year—fluctuations in our retirement accounts. The danger is that (1) we'll waste time and stress ourselves out needlessly, and (2) we'll be tempted to bail out when the market is down and buy when it's up.

This is really hard, I know. I'm sitting here writing this at 11:34 P.M. on August 4, 2011, and the Dow plunged more than 500 points today—its biggest one-day drop since 2008. Fear kicks in and your every instinct in this situation is stop the pain and sell. It is during times like these that you have to just reread this section. You have to be strong and force yourself to sit back, ignore the noise, and wait for the long-term trends that have driven the global economy upward for centuries.

The one good thing about all the media coverage and expert prognostication is that it lends itself wonderfully to mockery. Take this gem from CNBC.com:[12] "Stocks are at 'critical levels,' and if we continue to break through the current levels we could be in for further selling," said Art Cashin, director of floor operations at UBS Financial Services.

As far as I can tell, that literally means that if stocks continue to go down, they will continue to go down. It's absolutely meaningless. It's like saying "Well Jim, if the Red Sox continue to score runs, the scorekeeper's gonna keep putting up bigger numbers on the board."

Although come to think of it, that's actually probably something Tim McCarver has said.

My point is not to pick on Mr. Cashin. It's just that no one knows what's going to happen with the stock market in the short term, so when people try to predict they usually end up saying something pretty stupid.

A Harvard study found that the less frequently investors received information about the stock market, the better they performed.

This sounds insane, and possibly even dangerous. Be a better investor by buying mutual funds automatically and reading *Harry Potter* instead of the *Wall Street Journal*? But the research shows that access to greater amounts of financial news actually results in worse performance.

So by all means, follow the comings and goings of the financial world if you find it interesting or entertaining. That's what I do. But don't let it impact your investment decisions any more than you let *The Real Housewives* impact your spending decisions. Set up your automatic retirement investing so that money is taken out of your paycheck each month, invest in some index funds, and then go do something else. It sounds lazy and it is, but it's the best approach.

Why Investing Is the Best Tax Shelter in the World

The national pastime is baseball, but a close second is whining about income taxes.

But the higher the percentage of your wealth that comes from investments (as opposed to working) the less you'll pay in taxes.

This is incredibly regressive and may change somewhat but is unlikely ever to change entirely. Warren Buffett often points out that his receptionist pays a larger share of her income in taxes than he does—because her income is all from salary (lots of taxes) and his income comes basically exclusively from investments (very low taxes).

This is because when you have your money invested in assets that are going up in value—like the stock market, or real estate, or paintings of rectangles from the 1940s—*you don't pay any taxes until you decide to sell.* Your earnings can continue to compound year after year, whereas with ordinary income, you have to pay taxes on your gains at the end of every year. As I've already explained, the same is true for retirement plans, although your withdrawals will be taxed as ordinary income rather than as capital gains.

So, if you hate taxes, your best bet is to save up the money to buy index funds and then just hold them. Very little tax will be due as your money grows. Remember: Income from working = lots of taxes. Income from investing = very little or nothing in the way of taxes.

Socially Responsible Investing

Another option for your retirement investing—for those suckers among you who care about a better world and not just yourselves—is socially responsible investing.

Socially responsible mutual funds generally don't invest in weapons manufacturers, massive polluters, companies that sell tobacco or alcohol, or companies that mistreat their workers. (I disagree with the idea that companies that sell alcohol are socially irresponsible. Alcohol is responsible for the creation of far more lives than any other product on the market!) Other socially responsible funds manage money based on religious convictions. During the financial crisis, managers who invested based on Islamic law fared extremely well because the Koran's prohibition on the lending of money with interest led those investors to avoid investing in companies that were involved in subprime mortgages.[13]

The biggest of these socially responsible fund companies is Pax World Mutual Funds (PaxWorld.com). For people in their twenties and thirties, their Growth Fund is probably the best bet. The Vanguard FTSE Social Index Fund requires a minimum investment of

$3,000. If you have that much ready to start your Roth IRA, it's a great deal.

Interestingly, there is some research to suggest that socially responsible investing actually outperforms regular funds. The most socially progressive companies tend to attract the most progressive, creative people. And that can lead to success. Peter Camejo's book *The SRI Advantage: Why Socially Responsible Investing Has Outperformed Financially* makes the case for the benefits of socially responsible investing.

It makes some sense when you start to think about it. The business model of the tobacco industry literally involves killing all its customers on purpose. That's the business plan. How sustainable can that business be?

For the Love of Everything That's Holy, Please Don't Invest in Gold

If you're looking for a disaster-proof investment, gold doesn't strike me as a good bet. Certainly not any better than the dollar. Gold's long-term track record as an investment is poor and volatile, and characterized by run-ups in price followed by crashes. And over the long run, it's downright abysmal. In his book *Stocks for the Long Run*, Wharton professor Jeremy Siegel shows the long-term returns of different asset classes. One dollar invested in the stock market in 1802 would have been worth $12.7 million in 2006; $1 invested in bonds would have been worth $18,235. One dollar invested in gold would be worth $32.84. If looking at those statistics makes you go "HMM! I think I'll go put all my money in gold!" then there's not much hope for you. If you're young enough to have picked up this book, you're young enough to tolerate the potential volatility of investing your retirement assets in the stock market. The time when everyone's talking about gold is always the worst time to buy it. If you want to buy a little because you like it or because you've been listening to too many late-night infomercials, fine; but gold should not be a significant part of your retirement plan. Gold may have a role in the portfolio of older investors with lots of assets to invest. But for young people looking to save for retirement, it's not appropriate.

A few other oddball investment categories:

Guns and ammunition. I'm serious. (Which is to say, I'm largely not.) If all order breaks down—and the police aren't working because there is no functioning government because the dollar is worthless—owning a gun will be absolutely necessary to protect your family and your property. And, because most people don't own guns, you'll be able to barter items from your arsenal for just about anything you need. And with the economy collapsed, all the importing of raw materials that's necessary for gun production likely means that people won't be able to buy new guns. On a smaller budget—and with fewer storage and safety concerns—you can also just accumulate ammunition. And remember, with firearms as an asset class, your return on investment is really only limited by your willingness to use them.

Food. It sounds a little Unabomber, but there is nothing wrong with stockpiling some nonperishable food. Army surplus meals, canned goods, protein bars, that kind of thing. In the event of some sort of ridiculous political collapse (or natural disaster) that turns Manhattan into *Lord of the Flies*, this stuff will be a lot more valuable than most of the alternative investment classes you see being promoted in the media.

Fine art, rare books, wine, stamps, and so on. The luxury investments. They're snooty, sexy, sophisticated . . . and unlikely to be strong performers for you financially. I love art, and I buy rare books now and then, too—and when you're furnishing your home, buying stuff at good prices that will hold its value is something I encourage people to do. You have to furnish your home anyway—might as well make it look good. But for pure investment, the stock market is a much better idea.

Broadway shows. The best way to end up with a hundred dollars is to start with a billion dollars and invest it in Broadway shows. Ninety percent of Broadway shows lose money, but every once in a while one hits big. There are a number of funds that invest in Broadway shows based on complex formulas for predicting returns. These formulas mostly involve guessing. If theater is something that interests you, investing in it is definitely one of the more exiting ways to lose a bunch of money that you can afford to lose. Visit Bankrate.com (http://www.bankrate.com/brm/news/investing/20010730a.asp) for a great article on Broadway investing.

Limited edition collectibles, gold coins, sports cards, and so on. These are the sort of low-grade cousins of fine art and rare books: collectible plates, Beanie Babies, and commemorative gold coins hocked on late-night TV and talk radio. The technical term for the people who buy these is "suckers." Stay away from all of this stuff. If something is made to be collectible, it's virtually guaranteed to end up being worthless.

Save Your Next Two Raises

One of my friends recently changed jobs and it came with a 30 percent raise. He lives in New York City and earns less than $50,000 per year—and has a ton of student loan debt to pay off. Shortly after he got the new job, he posted on Facebook that he was "movin' on up" to a nicer apartment in a more expensive part of the city. This is not smart. If your income increases by 20 percent and you celebrate by increasing all your expenses by 20 percent, you will never get ahead.

It's just a mathematical impossibility. The key is to save your first two raises.

I'm not saying that if you start out earning $30,000 and eventually earn $500,000 per year, you live on $30,000 the whole time. That's not realistic and it's not fun. But, if you can manage not to increase your expenses after you take in your first two raises (diverting those raises straight into paying off debt or savings), you will have a *huge* leg up. You'll be able to increase your standard of living with subsequent salary hikes without straying from your plan.

Why Was This Section on Investing so Short?

A book on money that tells me to max out my 401(k) and Roth IRA and put as much money as possible into life-cycle index funds? What about short selling? What about options? What about bond funds? What exactly is a stock? Chances are, you already basically know what stocks are: They represent an ownership stake in a company. But, because I appreciate your young and eager minds, here's a quick breakdown of the rest of all that investing stuff:

> **Short selling.** This is a sophisticated strategy that allows you to profit from the decline of individual stocks, or from the market as a whole. Some of the smartest investment minds in the world have gotten rich doing it—people like Jim Chanos and David Einhorn. However, it's extremely dangerous and not something you should try.
> **Options.** Most of the above also applies here. Options are exciting, sophisticated, and chances are you will lose your money.
> **Bonds and bond funds.** Bonds are debt instruments. When you own a bond, the issuer of the bond owes you money. The value of the bond depends on interest rates and the chances that the issuer of the bond won't pay you back. Bonds issued

by the federal government are safest, but don't provide a high enough return for there to be any real reason for you to buy them. Just keep your money either in a life-cycle mutual fund or in a savings account.

All these things are interesting to some people (with the exception of bond funds, which are not interesting at all to anyone who doesn't have a personality disorder). But there is absolutely no benefit for most people, especially young people, in knowing about them. Your retirement savings should be invested in index funds. Once you have a very large amount of money in retirement, you may decide that you want to do some *exciting stuff*—that is, invest in places where you will almost certainly lose all your money. For an exploration of some of those possibilities—including Broadway shows, buying real estate over the phone, and more—check out Andrew Tobias's book *My Vast Fortune: The Money Adventures of a Quixotic Capitalist*. But don't get involved in that stuff until you have a net worth that is at least in the million-dollar range—and, even then, only with a small chunk of your assets.

Investing is that rare field where knowing a few basic things can often serve you better than knowing a lot. Because the more you know, the more tempted you may be to try something fancy—or to compete with others who know even more. In investing, simplicity beats complexity. As Dave Ramsey has said, "Simple plans create millionaires."

So here's the simple plan: Contribute up to the maximum match in your 401(k), investing that money in stock market index funds or a target date retirement fund. If you can contribute even more, set up a Roth IRA with a discount brokerage like Vanguard, invested in index funds. Set this up so that you automatically pay yourself first each month. Then, if you still have money left over to save for retirement, go back and continue to invest in the 401(k). And then go do something else, like Zumba.

Spend Less, Live More, Be Happier, but Don't Get Asked to Appear on *Hoarders* Too Often

Spending

> Never keep up with the Joneses. Drag them down to your level.
> It's cheaper.
>
> —QUENTIN CRISP

If you have a problem with excessive spending—and most people do—blame your parents.

As teenagers, Gen Y shoppers spend about five times as much as their parents did—*after* adjusting for inflation.[1] Although the United States comprises only 4.5 percent of the global population, we consume 45 percent of the world's toys.[2] American parents give their kids more in allowance money each year than the half a billion poorest adults on the planet earn.[3] No wonder we want a lot of stuff when we get older. The problem is that, once we get out of our parents' house and into the workforce of the 2010s, our inflation-adjusted incomes are actually lower than our parents'. And that's if we can find full-time jobs.

There's also a fairly large chunk of the population that has a psychological problem with over-shopping. A 2006 study conducted by the Stanford University School of Medicine (a prestigious medical school, so you know the study is automatically valid) found that 5.8 percent of Americans are compulsive over-shoppers. That's more than 17 million people.[4]

Researchers Susan Fournier and Michael Guiry found that 61 percent of respondents "always have something in mind that [they] look forward to buying." Twenty-seven percent said that they "dream about things they do not own" very frequently.[5]

When you're brought up spending five times as much as your parents did and are conditioned to see "stuff" as an important social self-identity marker, but earn less money than your parents did—at least in the short term—you have a problem.

So something has to give: our spending or our saving. If you're reading this, I'm assuming you don't see giving up on your financial life as an option.

But people are bored of hearing about spending less. In recent years, there's been what I would call a latte backlash.

Quite a few years ago, personal finance experts—perhaps most notably David Bach, who actually trademarked the phrase "Latte Factor"—started telling people that the difference between wealth and poverty lies in relatively small purchases.

Skip little luxuries, like lattes, we're told, and you'll end up rich.

It all sounded too good to be true, and pretty soon a bunch of gurus started mocking it. One personal finance book published in 2010 promised that you could "have your latte and drink it, too!"

But actually, if from age twenty to age sixty-five you take the $5 per day spent on little luxuries and invest it in a mutual fund at an average annual return of 10 percent, you'll end up with nearly $1.4 million.

In other words, you *can* actually end up rich just by cutting out your lattes. Although forty-five years from now a latte could cost $100.

Ben Franklin had it right when he said "Beware of little expenses: a small leak will sink a great ship." This is not to say that you shouldn't drink lattes; it's just that you absolutely must save a good chunk of your income, and the difference between saving enough to end up secure and not saving anything at all is pretty small if you look at it in terms of daily expenses.

Why This Book Contains No Budgeting Forms

If you've read other personal finance books, you may have noticed something strange about this one by now: There are no budgeting forms for you to fill in, nor any stern admonitions to track all of your spending or set rules about how much you should spend on everything.

Here's why: (1) that stuff just isn't any fun to write about; (2) that stuff just isn't any fun to read about; (3) even if I told you to "Get on a budget!" I doubt you'd listen; (4) making a budget doesn't mean you'd stick to it anyway, and (5) most of the smartest, most frugal money managers on the planet don't use budgets (see below).

Many people do find budgeting to be a useful organizing principle for their financial lives. If you're one of them, there are some great websites and free or close to free computer programs that can help. Mint.com is great, as is the program offered by YouNeeda Budget.com.

Another program that is great—largely because of its simplicity—is Dave Ramsey's Envelope System. It's a paper- and cash-based system, and it costs $19.95 on his website. It's totally worth it if you're struggling with months that last longer than your money. You can order it here: http://www.daveramsey.com/store/prod210.html.

I don't use any of these programs and, interestingly, neither do most of the best home economists out there. Jeff Yeager talked to a lot of personal finance superstars for his book *The Cheapskate Next*

Door, and he reports that "contrary to what non-cheapskates seem to think, only about 10 percent of the cheapskates polled said that they have a formal, written household budget. For most of us, a budget seems too much like a diet: a plan that's always looming over you, bringing you down, when what you really need is a lasting lifestyle change that makes the desired behavior effortless."

In an e-mail, Yeager told me that most people who manage their money well come to view frugality as the obvious and right way to live. "These are folks who have really internalized their budgets, and for whom smart spending has become second nature," he wrote. "As one [cheapskate] told me, 'We live our budget; we don't waste time writing about it.'"

To get you on a frugal path, I want to help you change the way you think about money. Most people only have the self-discipline to force themselves to do things for limited periods of time. But if you can learn how to think about money the right way, you will have the formula for lasting change.

Which brings me back to budgets one last time. As Yeager explained, "A number of my cheapskates talked about having financial problems at some point in the past, and using a strict, written budget early on to get their financial house in order (particularly when digging out of debt). But once they got on top of their situations, the need for a formal budget disappeared as they made smart-spending a force of habit. And I think that's a very hopeful thing for people who are facing financial problems and have this sense of doom and gloom, expecting that for the rest of their lives they'll have a budget spreadsheet tattooed to their ass. Not so, says the cheapskate next door."

Need help with sticking to your efforts to cut back spending? One great site for this is StickK.com. Founded by Yale economists Ian Ayres and Dean Karlan, along with graduate student Jordan Goldberg, StickK.com lets you set up a goal—and then encourages you to stick with it.

When you set up your goal, you establish consequences for

yourself if you don't stick with it. You can either hold yourself accountable or ask a friend to keep an eye on you, and then you report your progress to the site, which will enforce the consequences you set up. For example, if you don't pay off your credit card by the end of the month, you might set it up so that StickK.com sends a $10 donation to the Thomas Kinkade Foundation.

So by all means, if you find it helpful, set up a budget and decide how much you can afford to spend in each category (the six basic categories are food, shelter, transportation, retirement, paying down debt, and court-ordered victim restitution) and then spend it. If you like doing this, you can also set up long-term goals and save for those, too. And if you want to get really fancy, you can even set up special sub-savings accounts at your banks so that you have one account for "wedding," one for "mom's birthday present," and another for "paternity test." Then, you can arrange to have a portion of every check you deposit automatically split off into each account. This isn't how I manage my own money and I don't actually know anyone who does this, either, so I'm not going to write about it any further.

Now comes the fun part: looking at the different ways of spending money, and choosing the smart ones.

Keeping Up with the Jonestown: The Financial Suicide of Competitive Consumption

> A man is rich in proportion to the number of things he can do without.
>
> —HENRY DAVID THOREAU

A significant part of the spending most people do consists of competitive consumption—an effort to keep up with the lifestyles and trappings of their friends and, more dangerously, people they see on

TV. If your plan is to be the next Teresa Giudice, you're gonna have a problem.

I often hear this lamented as a uniquely American problem, or a recent one. But the truth is, as long as humans have had money, we've been spending it in ways designed to try to make other people feel insecure. In the 1600s, wealthy Italians built luxurious palaces and then placed tiles in the facade that said *pro invidia*—to be envied. In eighteenth-century England, laws were passed to forbid people who weren't wealthy from trying to dress like the wealthy— if we brought these laws back, by the way, credit card debt in the United States would likely fall by 18.7 percent, according to calculations I just made up. In her book *The Overspent American*, Juliet B. Schor reports that "at the turn of the century, the wealthy published menus of their dinner parties in the newspapers"—for the sole purpose of making the lower classes feel jealous. Of course, there was also a part of American history when women were considered property, slave trader was near the top of *U.S. News & World Report's* guide to "10 Booming Careers!," and the best thing people could find to smoke was opium. We've progressed in a lot of areas, but the desire to show off with possessions is not one of them.

Back then, with the lines between the upper and lower classes clear cut, it was far more difficult to pretend you were wealthy if you weren't. And they didn't know about leasing BMWs. As more and more people have acquired disposable income, it's much easier to blow money on things that make you feel wealthier than you are. But most of the people who do are frauds. To demonstrate this, researcher Robert Kelly observed people on a tour bus arriving at a museum. "Upon being discharged from the tour bus, [one-third of visitors] entered the museum foyer, searched for and found the museum shop, purchased some object . . . and then returned to their bus without ever entering the museum galleries."[6]

Here are some tips on how to resist the urge to consume conspicuously:

Realize that the people who look rich aren't. As Thomas J. Stanley showed in his book *Stop Acting Rich*, the most popular car among millionaires is the Toyota. They also tend to wear Timex watches and drink lower-end wine. If you want to look like a millionaire, buy stuff you can afford. That's why millionaires do it and if you do it for a while, you will become one of them.

Do some "internal calculations" to show that if you really wanted to, you could buy all that crap your friends have. There's a certain natural competitive streak in most people. I'm not going to lie, driving an older, low-end car (like I do) can sometimes make you feel like a loser when it seems like everyone else is posting pictures of their BMWs on Facebook. But running the numbers and knowing that, if you really wanted something like that you could afford it, can overcome the desire to consume competitively. It's like going to a cheap school because you got rejected by Tulane, versus going there even though you *were* accepted to Tulane. Knowing you *could* have gone there—that you were good enough but chose to spend your money more wisely—can make you feel good about not going instead of bad.

Try to picture the invisible status symbols. The whole problem of conspicuous consumption would be solved if we had a law that required license plates to display the owner's monthly car payments, and couture clothes came with the wearer's credit report and last five years' worth of tax returns stapled to the front. But failing that, you just have to picture it.

Pay attention to your reference group. Researcher Juliet B. Schor found that people who identify their lifestyle reference group as those with higher incomes than their own are more likely to save less money and accumulate more debt. Your reference group is basically the group you compare your own lifestyle to: a combination of friends, relatives, acquaintances, and "celebutards." This is a fantastic reason to avoid watching *Keeping Up with the Kardashians*. Schor found that, for instance, every hour of television viewing per week above the norm correlates with a reduction in savings of $208 per year. Every step above their reference group that people were in terms of income correlated with increased savings of $2,953 per year. Surrounding yourself with people who earn less and spend less than you is one of the most powerful things you can do to improve your financial life. If you want to be rich, get yourself some poor friends.

Ask yourself what void you're looking to fill with the money you're spending. There are some purchases that, although extravagant, might very well generate a strong happiness return because they are particular to *your* interests and who *you* are. If you love to play the violin, buying an expensive, high-quality violin can bring you happiness every single time you play it for decades. But if your spending is motivated by a more extrinsic need—fitting in, looking cool, crafting the right image—you absolutely have to know that spending money will not give you the happiness boost that you're looking for. So ask yourself: Why am I buying this? And then look to find other ways to fill that need that don't involve spending money. **Calculate the expenditure in terms of how much you earn per hour.** And ask yourself if it's worth it. If I earn $8 an hour after-tax and this sweater costs $40, is it worth five hours of my time? As Henry David Thoreau said: "The price of anything is the amount of life you exchange for it." Looking at your financial decisions in terms of the chunk of life you're exchanging for stuff will tell you a lot about your values, and help you figure out how to align your financial life with your moral and spiritual life. Vicki Robin and Joe Dominguez's *Your Money or Your Life* is an excellent book that expands on this idea.

Beautiful Dirty Retailer Tricks

A bargain is something you can't use at a price you can't resist.

—FRANKLIN P. JONES

It used to be that marketers looked to appeal to our tastes; they'd ask us what we value and try to market to us based on that using focus groups and surveys.

Now they go deeper, trying to figure out all the subconscious cues that cause us to spend money and play to those instead. This is warfare, and marketers are worthy foes, especially when consumers are uninformed. I was recently in GNC checking out a 20-percent-off sale; they had a sign promoting the savings. The sign showed a table: Twenty percent off a $10 purchase means you save $2. Twenty percent off a $50 purchase means you save $10—right on up to the savings on a couple hundred dollars' worth of protein bars and pills that speed up your metabolism at the possible expense of a heart attack.

Now granted, this ad was probably mostly intended for the juice-head element of GNC's customer base ("Yo! Bro! What's 20 percent of $10?"), but think about it: What match are consumers who have trouble calculating percentages for a multi-hundreds-of-billions-of-dollars marketing industry?

Here are some of the marketing tactics retailers use to trick you into overpaying and buying stuff you probably don't even really want:

"Sincere" flattery. I was once shopping for a suit to wear to a job interview. I hate wearing suits and I especially hate wearing boring suits, so I went into Express and found what I thought was a really hot seersucker suit. I tried it on (with a brown shirt and fabulous purple tie) and the salesperson said, "It's a great look, and it works for you. I would tell a lot of other people that it was too flashy, but it's good on you." So I bought it and wore it to the job interview. When I got home, I had an e-mail from a friend who worked there: "You wore a [expletive] seersucker suit in here? With a [expletive] purple tie?" In other words, the suit was enough of a mistake that it was the most memorable part of my interview. I later learned that flattery combined with a caveat of "I would tell most people not to buy this" is a very popular trick in retailing these days because consumers are so used to flattery that it no longer works. So this sort of sincere flattery—which is actually even more manipulative than traditional flattery—is something to look out for.

Low opening price points. Walmart is famous for this. They'll have one really, really low-priced item in a category—like televisions—but it will be an off-brand of questionable reliability. Yet the fact that that item is cheaper than what you'd be able to find at any other store will make you think the better models will be similarly good values—but often, that's not the case. Comparison shopping is the only way to know whether the price you see is a good deal. For those of you with smartphones, there are a bunch of comparison shopping apps that people seem to like. ShopSavvy is a free one that lets you scan the barcode on an item and then it compares it to tons of other online stores.

Having one really expensive item to make everything else look cheaper. In a piece in *New York* magazine, William Poundstone (the author of *Priceless: The Myth of Fair Value [and How to Take Advantage of It]*) dissected the menu of a New York City restaurant that had one item that was far more expensive than the rest. He explained that the only reason that the $115 platter was on the menu was to make everything else look cheaper by comparison. When a restaurant or store offers us a $500 option, we suddenly feel frugal for buying the $150 option instead—even if the $150 option is not a particularly good deal.

Meaningless sales. I once saw a sign that said "MEN'S SUITS! UP TO 30% OFF OR MORE." This is an ad that catches your eye, but if you actually think about it, it means literally nothing. It means that the suits are up to 30 percent off—that is, they could be full price—or more—and they could be free; in fact, they might even be paying you to take the suits off their hands. No matter what store you're in, everything is always up to 30 percent off or more. Retailers do this all the time; just because a sale is advertised doesn't mean you'll actually find bargains.

How to Shop

A study published in the *Journal of Marketing Research* found that, on average, men spend more money when they shop with a friend; women spend the same amount of money whether accompanied or alone.[7] So guys, please try to resist the urge to head over to Bath & Body Works with your frat brothers; I don't want peer pressure tempting you to stock up on more Sweet Pea candles than you can afford, even if they are on sale.

When it comes to shopping online, I'm of two minds. It's indisputable that many of the best bargains in shopping can be found online. But for too many people, online shopping becomes an all-consuming pastime. According to a survey conducted by *China Youth Daily*, 71 percent of Chinese young adults thought they had "online shopping addiction," 25.6 percent thought they were seriously addicted, and 45.5 percent thought they were "somewhat addicted."[8]

If you find yourself inclined toward excessive online spending, stick with brick and mortar. The somewhat higher prices you might pay will be outweighed by the fact that you'll be shopping less frequently (and things may fit better).

Oh! And in physical stores you can pay with cash.

Stanford psychiatrist Elias Aboujaoude sees something more sinister at work in online shopping: a destructive outlet for the self-absorption that the Internet encourages. "The Internet and related technologies have turned money into an even less tangible and further removed concept than the plastic of credit cards, and that is having real repercussions on our personal and national financial health," he wrote in *Psychology Today*. "Fueled by grandiose, narcissistic, and impulsive notions, it is easier online to feel as special, deserving, and immune to bankruptcy as a Marie Antoinette—and to shop accordingly."[9]

Online shopping is a great way to find the best deal when you're looking for something, but avoid having it mushroom into a pattern of compulsive overspending. Don't sign up to receive e-mails about daily deals, or you'll end up like most people who use these deal sites: lonely with a closet full of crap you don't even want.

How to Negotiate Anything (or, How I Smashed a Hotel Room Phone and Talked Them Out of Making Me Pay for It)

Even as I write this, I'm not really sure it's a good idea. I'm about to tell you the story of what is probably the most embarrassing thing I've ever done, so please don't judge me.

I once checked into a hotel after an incredibly annoying day. I went to check my e-mail, and the Internet wasn't working. I picked up the phone to report it and couldn't reach anyone and then, in an act of great maturity, I threw the phone. I don't remember having thrown it that hard, but it completely shattered—the explosion probably would have looked really cool in slow motion. Could've been a big viral hit on YouTube.

The only time I've ever broken anything in a fit of rage in my life; and it had to be a hotel room phone. I instantly surveyed my options: I could try to hide the phone and hope they didn't find it or I could stuff it in my bag and take it off-site.

I'm not gonna lie: Both of those options really did pop into my head. I even thought about trying to escape through the hotel room window. But ultimately I decided to do the right thing, just to mix it up a little. So I headed down to the check-in desk.

"Hey, I got a new one for ya!" I told the clerk in my cheeriest voice.

"Uh-oh," he replied, instantly looking up.

"So here's the thing," I said, still smiling. "I had a horrible night last night and I broke one of the phones in the room."

"Broke it? Like, smashed it?"

"Yes, into several pieces."

"Too much to drink?"

"No actually, completely sober. I think if I'd had a couple drinks, that phone would still be intact."

I asked how much it would cost to replace it and he looked it up in the computer: $68.

At this point, I decided that I was going to try to talk him into not charging me at all to replace the phone.

I did not have a leg to stand on, but why should that stop me?

The manager, who looked kind of like Snooki after a "dress for success" makeover and a three-month binge of Miss Manners columns, came out and I said, "Ah! You couldn't resist the opportunity to meet the lunatic!"

She laughed and said, "Nah, it happens more than you'd think!"

"Really?"

"Yeah, I have a theory: Men smash stuff over money, and women smash stuff over men."

This is, by the way, the greatest insight into humanity that I've ever heard—and it came from a hotel manager.

"So if you check the news and see the stock market plunging, you instantly call your distributor and are like 'We're gonna need another thirty flat-screen televisions!'?"

"Basically."

"So here's the thing: This is the first time I've ever done anything like this. I've stayed in this hotel before, I really like staying here, and I would really, really appreciate it if you could help me out on this."

She laughed. "Yeah. I really appreciate your honesty. Most people who break stuff either try to hide it or take it with them and think we won't notice. But we do notice. And, by the way, we normally charge a $200 fee for any damage plus the cost of the replacement. I'm just going to waive this whole thing. Hope today is a better day for you."

And that is how easy it was. Here are some of my rules for negotiating:

In most cases, negotiations are much more about building rapport than being right. When you call customer service— or talk to a clerk in a store—you are most likely going to deal with a paid-by-the-hour person who talks with a lot of people who are rude and obnoxious. My mother, a therapist, has a saying: "You can say almost anything to almost anyone if you phrase it right." Be nice, be goofy, be self-deprecating, and try to make the person laugh. If he likes you, he may be willing to bend a little to get something done. If the person doesn't like you, he is likely to deny even the most reasonable request just because he can. Be nice. You're not superstar sports agent Scott Boras negotiating a $150 million contract for some steroid-shooting slugger. You *need* the person on the other end of the transaction to like you.

Always be honest. The manager told me that the hotel normally charges a $200 fee for any damage to a room, plus the cost of replacement. But she said that I was the first person in a long time to walk up to the desk and announce that I had broken something. Customer service people are lied to all the freakin' time and you're probably not as slick as you think: They're gonna know that you're lying. Just tell the truth, admit to being an idiot, and ask them to cut you a deal anyway. You'll feel better about yourself and it has at least as good of a chance at working as trying to BS your way into savings.

Avoid yes or no questions. When you say "Can you give me a discount?" or "Will you waive that fee?" you are making it very easy for him or her to just say, "Sorry, no." But when you ask, "What can you do to help me with this situation?" it's much more difficult for the other person to say, "There is absolutely nothing I can do to help you with this situation." Vague queries often lead to better results than explicit demands that can be too easily shot down.

Almost anything is worth negotiating. If you can smash a hotel room phone and then talk your way out of paying for it, you can negotiate almost anything. When you're making a significant purchase—whether it's a new television, a car, a house, or a gym membership—it's worth trying to get a lower price.

Establish yourself as a long-term customer. If you're trying to negotiate with a bank to get them to waive an overdraft fee: "I'm a long-term customer, I have multiple accounts with you, I'm generally thrilled with the service, and I would hate for our relationship to be over because of a $25 fee," will often do the trick. Banks spend, on average, about $350 on marketing and administrative costs for every customer that they acquire. This is true in many other industries as well. Once they have you as a customer, it is economically much better for them to give up $15, $25, or $100 than to spend $350 to recruit another customer to replace you. And with so many banks to choose from and so many online options, banks know you really can ditch them if you want to.

Always try to negotiate with small businesses. Mom-and-pop stores generally have much greater leeway for negotiating—you'll generally have no problem finding someone to talk to who has the authority to do everything from giving you a 10 percent discount to giving you an item for free. But increasingly, it's possible to haggle at even the biggest of big box stores as well. Can't hurt to try.

Talk to someone really high up. Everyone knows you should try to speak with a supervisor. But it can also be a good idea to write to the chief executive officer (CEO)—or another senior official whose contact information you can find on the company's website. Often, you're actually better off going with someone in the middle. Warren Buffett is unlikely to intervene for you, but an executive vice president or a regional director might.

Go complain online. This method tends to get abused, and it can very quickly deteriorate into extortion and libel. But if you have a legitimate complaint and aren't getting anywhere with the company, posting about it on Twitter or a blog can be a good way to get the company's attention because companies hate seeing bad stuff about themselves on the Internet. Note: This won't work with big banks because approximately 87 percent of people have made a YouTube video about how much they hate Citigroup. In 2009, a guy got in a feud with United Airlines after his expensive guitar was broken on a plane and the company refused to do anything about it. His music video "United Breaks Guitars" got more than ten million views and brought United Airlines back to the negotiating table. My favorite lines in the song are: "You broke it, you should fix it / You're liable, just admit it / I should've flown with someone else / Or gone by car."

If you try the nice guy route and find yourself dealing with a complete jerk, here's what I recommend—and I only endorse doing this if you really are dealing with a complete jerk. Ask the customer service person for his or her work e-mail address, and then sign him or her up for tons of daily e-mails: vegan cooking tips, cribbage puzzles, "How to Live with Gonorrhea," and "Life After Bankruptcy." OK, don't really do that.

Mostly Legal Ways to Save Money on Everything

Being alive costs a lot of money. Between alcohol, Uggs, microwavable meals, and iTunes, it can be hard to get ahead financially. Here are some tips on how to save money on almost everything.

Wine

As Kenny Rogers sang, "The cheaper the grapes are, the sweeter the taste of the wine." Wine connoisseurs annoy me more than just about any other group of people on the planet. It isn't wine that bothers me, it's the incessant yammering about vintages, viticulture, aperitifs, jeroboams, oenology, and sommeliers.

I once went on a date with this very pretentious guy in Miami Beach. We went to an equally pretentious "wine bar" where you took a glass, put it below a spigot, inserted a card (that was linked to the credit/debit card you presented when you arrived at the restaurant), and out poured a sip-sized serving of an expensive wine.

All this for the low, low, introductory price of anywhere from $3 to $11 per sip.

The guy, we'll call him Mr. Smug, would take a sip, swirl it, and then sniff it like some ancient voodoo shaman sniffing urine to detect for signs of illness. Then he'd make some sort of pronouncement like "Ah! This has cedar overtones."

I have never wanted to disembowel someone so badly in my life. I thought he was full of crap and it turns out that he probably was. In 2008, researchers at Yale, along with the help of some Swedish economists, looked at the results from thousands of blind taste tests and found that, on average, people actually prefer cheaper wines to more expensive ones.[10]

Another study is perhaps even funnier. Frédéric Brochet, a researcher at the University of Bordeaux, invited fifty-seven internationally recognized wine experts to evaluate two different kinds of wine: a red wine and a white wine. The experts described the red wine as "intense," "deep," and "spicy"—words that are often used to describe red wines—and they described the white wine as "lively," "fresh," and "floral." None of the experts picked up on the fact that they were the *exact same wine*. The clever Dr. Brochet had simply colored one of them with food coloring. They were both white wine.[11]

Interestingly, this research is not without precedent: Researchers at the University of Pennsylvania's Annenberg School for Communication found that when cereal was placed into a box with a picture of an animal on it, children responded by giving it better ratings in a taste test.

The difference is that five-year-olds who like Tony the Tiger don't have clubs and magazines where they talk about cereal.[12] Also, they're five. So shut up with your stupid wine talk. You're not fooling anyone.

Now, since many of us are unfortunate enough to run in circles where some people obsess over wine (I've tried to jettison as many of my wine aficionado friends as possible, but a few have managed to stick around), here are a few tips:

> **To make it sound like you know about wine, announce that you detect a "hint of elderberry overtones."** No one knows what elderberry tastes like but he or she will assume that you do and therefore think you are smart and sophisticated. I got this tip from my uncle, a former professional wine salesman, and I've tested it at parties. It works wonderfully and people will think you know what you're talking about.

Never buy Italian wines. Eduardo Porter, a *New York Times* economics reporter and the author of *The Price of Everything: Solving the Mystery of Why We Pay What We Do*, writes that "Americans will pay more for a French wine than an Argentine wine of similar quality, the same grape varietal [Yeah, I don't know what that means, either], and the same age. Simply stamping 'Product of Italy' on the label can raise the price of a bottle by more than 50 percent."

If you have a party, serve crappy discount store wine but casually leave a couple of copies of *Wine Spectator* on the living room table. It'll cost you $5.95 if you buy it at a bookstore, but you also might be able to find it—or magazines like it—at a thrift shop or library book sale. People will note that you have wine magazines and therefore assume that you're serving expensive wine.

Try to find open-bar events in your area. Alcohol is expensive even when you buy it at home but it's nothing compared to the prices you'll pay in bars, especially in hot urban areas. One solution to this is to try to find open-bar events in your area—or wine tastings, gallery openings, that kind of thing. If you live in an area with a vibrant social life, there are tons of opportunities to drink on someone else's dime. If you live in New York City, MyOpenBar.com has a calendar featuring opportunities to get free drinks each night. (The site is planning to expand to other cities as well.) Otherwise, check events sites, Craigslist, local sites like Patch.com, and even, gasp, local newspapers.

Don't get drunk at office holiday parties. I am a big proponent of free alcohol. This enthusiasm does not carry over to work situations. If you work for a company, there is a good chance it has an office party for the holidays. There is also a good chance that said party is open bar. Office party high jinks are such a common source of career disasters that the management book *101 Sample Write-Ups for Documenting Employee Performance Problems: A Guide to Progressive Discipline & Termination* (I swear this book exists) actually has a sample form to be used for terminating an employee for "Summary Discharge: Misconduct at Company Holiday Party," with sample legalese like "This employee became very drunk, lifted her skirt to male employees whom she found attractive, and attempted to place several men's hands on her breasts. The supervisor chose not to describe these actions in detail in this letter for the sake of propriety." Also for the sake of propriety: Have one or two drinks at your office party, but do not sacrifice your career at the altar of free booze; yes, I'm talking to you, Mel Gibson.

Clothing

> Be wary of any enterprise that requires new clothes.
>
> —HENRY DAVID THOREAU

Avoiding the urge to spend excessively on clothing used to be easier—mainly because you'd be jailed or flogged on the village green if you didn't. In my home state of Massachusetts in 1634, the General Court banned colonists from buying clothing of "great, superfluous, unnecessary expense." Five years later, lace was banned for contributing to the "nourishing of pride and the exhausting of men's estates, and also of evil example to others."

In an effort to preserve the economic hierarchy, laws were even tougher on the lower classes. Only people with net worths of more than 200 pounds were allowed to wear certain expensive fabrics; everyone else would be fined ten shillings per violation.

Today you can wear whatever you want, which is a problem because a lot of people are going broke from it.

It seems, when I look around, that there are basically two kinds of people when it comes to clothing: those who run up fashion debt and those whose fashion icon is Michael Moore.

Both of these are bad ideas. Rob Nelissen and Marijn Meijers, social psychologists at Tilburg University in the Netherlands, conducted a few experiments to find out whether brand of clothing effects how people are perceived. *Time* magazine reported that "Nelissen and Meijers showed volunteers one of two videos of the same man being interviewed for a job. In one video his shirt featured a logo and in the other it didn't. Volunteers rated him more suitable for the position, and suggested he earn 9 percent more, when a conspicuous logo was present."[13]

"The present data suggest that luxury consumption can be a profitable social strategy because conspicuous displays of luxury qualify as a costly signaling trait that elicits status-dependent favorable treatment in human social interactions," the authors noted.

Others are not so sure. Celebrity stylist Phillip Bloch, author of *The Shopping Diet: Spend Less and Get More*, says that as an employer, he tends to frown on people who show up at job interviews decked out in designer threads.

And Bloch is someone you should pay attention to. He's styled Halle Berry, Drew Barrymore, Michael Jackson, Will Smith, John Travolta, and Nicole Kidman—which, last I checked, is a more impressive client list than the aunt who's always talking about all the couture she owns.

"Don't over-label; you're not impressing the boss," Bloch told me. "In general, you don't want to look like a label-whore. It conveys an image of *trying too hard* and it makes you look high maintenance."

And especially outside of the workplace, Bloch advises young people to avoid designer clothing. "What's sexier is having personal style," he says. "You can't buy good taste. Just because you're putting on a pair of Dolce & Gabbana sunglasses doesn't mean you're classy. It's not the case. The main problem is that people are hiding behind the labels as opposed to showing what they really are. What's really hot is all those kids who are shopping and putting together great looks are using their style and not hiding behind a brand."

So be very careful: Wearing a button-down with a Ralph Lauren logo on it during an interview might make a good impression. But that's really the extent of it; don't go crazy with labels.

But that does not mean you should dress like a hobo. Unless your career and social life consist exclusively of sitting at home alone, there's a high price to pay for not looking good. A Yahoo! HotJobs survey found that 82 percent of human resources employees believe appearance can affect getting promoted. One study looked at job interviews in the United States and Canada and found that applicants who were identified by the interviewer as being below average in beauty earned about 7 percent less than the average, whereas those who were above average in terms of attractiveness made 5 percent more.

So, take care of your body—and make sure you look good. Your physical appearance might very well be a better career investment than a graduate degree. Join a gym, stop bingeing on Hot Pockets at 3:00 A.M., and drink more water.

Some tips on shopping:

Clean your freakin' closet. "The best place to shop is your closet," says Bloch. "Clean out your closet so you know what you have, get rid of the crap, and try on *everything*. Cleaning out your closet, organizing it, and finding out what actually works will make you look better *and* save you money."

"Elegance is elimination." "Fifteen pieces you wear all the time is a lot better than fifty pieces you can't find anything to go with and don't know where to wear," Bloch says. A good wardrobe is about having a few classics that will go with everything, and then enough other pieces to accessorize with them and create wonderful outfits. It's not about having five hundred pairs of shoes.

Maybe it is about having five hundred pairs of shoes. If you wear a pair of shoes a lot, they won't last. So when it comes to shoes I buy a lot of them—but only when they're on sale at stores like Marshalls. And only styles that will always look good. This is the Zac Shoe Theorem: The more shoes you own, the longer each pair will last so the marginal cost of new shoes is close to zero. Looking good is an investment. As one friend recently argued about the heels she'd just purchased: "With these shoes, I could stand on a street corner and have them paid for in like twenty minutes!" Now that's economizing.

Take care of your clothes. Mrs. Clean, a housekeeping company in Seattle, suggests that only underwear, towels, sheets, bathrobes, and bath mats should be washed in hot water.[14] Laundry detergents are so much better and so much more powerful today than they were fifty years ago that many of the old rules about using hot water don't apply. Not only is it cheaper to wash your clothes in warm or even cold water but also it will help them last longer.

Don't buy the whole "buy quality for the long-term" argument. One of my favorite nonsense arguments for buying expensive clothes is that "they last longer!" Here's the thing: Clothes are much more likely to wear out from improper care or other issues that are unrelated to quality. Bright white Abercrombie & Fitch T-shirts do not have some special ability to emerge unscathed when you dump a liter of Bloody Mary mix on them. I know of what I speak.

Buy used. There are few better ways to cut the cost of clothing than by buying items that are gently used. Thrift shops like the Salvation Army and Goodwill are probably not the way to go.

Yes, stuff turns up there but you have to kiss a lot of frogs. Instead, try smaller local thrift shops and consignment shops like Plato's Closet and Buffalo Exchange. eBay can also be a source of bargains. The other nice thing about buying used? You don't have to worry about what the clothing will look like once it shrinks in the wash because it comes preshrunk!

Buy in season. Retailers generally market clothes for the coming season, not the current season. One of my favorite personal finance experts is Clark Howard, and he says, "Wait until the first day that actually fits the season that the clothes were being sold for, and then you buy it. So September 21 is when you buy fall wardrobe because then it's on clearance because they're putting all the winter stuff in. You wear the clothes once the season's upon you. Not when the retailers tell you."[15]

The Internet is your friend! "Nowadays, more than ever, you don't have to spend the big money to get big style," Phillip Bloch says. "There's so many places to find great clothes at a great price." His two favorite sites for finding deals? ShopItToMe.com and BeyondTheRack.com.

Find off-brands that fit you really well. Any fashionista will tell you that what really matters is not so much the *quality* of the clothing—or even the color—but how it *fits* your body. Try going to an affordable store—Target, Walmart, T.J. Maxx, and so on—and try on a few of the off-brands of T-shirts that they regularly have in large quantities. Find one that fits you well, and stock up. Ditto for jeans, button-downs, and polos.

Avoid the trend pieces. Bloch told me that one of the most important rules of fashion is to absolutely never buy the hot new thing that you keep seeing in all the magazines. Remember when Ashton Kutcher started wearing Von Dutch trucker hats, and then pretty soon every other bed wetter with a twelve-inch TV and a PacSun within thirty miles started wearing trucker hats? Yeah, don't buy those.

Buy children's sizes. If you have a small build, you should absolutely try on clothing at the children's equivalents of your favorite stores. You can save a ton of money this way. For instance, an XL Abercrombie & Fitch kid's T-shirt retails for $19.50. A comparable adult version retails for $40. This won't work for all sizes, but if you have a lean, slightly muscular build, the tighter-fitting kid sizes actually can make you look better and save you money. Fair warning: If you're going to try this, cut the tags out before you get involved in any situation where you might end up taking off your clothes with someone else present. Unless you're R. Kelly, there is nothing less hot or more creepy than ripping off someone's shirt to see a Gap Kids label.

A little bit of talent is worth a lot of money. If you don't have a great eye for fashion, consider finding a friend who will do your shopping with you, on your budget, and will help you put together looks that work for you. If you don't have any fashionable friends (or they have better things to do than go shopping with you), go online. One of my favorite fashion websites is PennyChic.com, which features the fashion successes of a professional stylist, who puts her looks together exclusively at Walmart. Consider her your fashion virtual friend: She shows you how to style with Walmart and then you can go to the store and put it together for yourself.

Scour the clearance racks—with an eye toward resale! This is only worth doing if you really love clothing and consider shopping to be your hobby. Kathy Spencer, author of *How to Shop for Free*, scores deals like $15 cashmere sweaters on clearance at mall stores . . . and then sells them on eBay for several times what she paid.

Clothing swaps. Swaporamarama.org offers nationwide listings of clothing swaps. I don't really like the idea of doing

them with friends because of the potential for awkwardness
("Sorry, Jeremy! I guess we can't swap clothes because your
fat thighs ain't gonna fit in my Lucky Brand jeans"), but
some people do.

Nothing Tastes as Good as Skinny Feels

Everybody wanna be a big-ass bodybuilder but don't nobody
wanna lift no heavy-ass weights.

—RONNIE COLEMAN, BODYBUILDER

The word *aerobics* came about when the gym instructors got
together and said, "If we're going to charge $10 an hour, we can't
call it jumping up and down."

—RITA RUDNER

A big part of being better-looking than your parents is keeping your
body in shape. This will also come in handy in the event that you
need to fight them.

And, like dressing well, being fit can actually help your career.
A University of Helsinki study found that, on average, obese women
earn 30 percent less than women of normal weight.[16] "Being overweight can be dangerous to your wealth," Jay L. Zagorsky, an economist at Ohio State University, told the *New York Times*.[17]

Exercise has numerous other benefits. According to Daniel
Landers of Arizona State University, aside from helping maintain
general health, exercise can also help you reduce anxiety, reduce
depression, build self-esteem, and help you sleep better.[18]

But being in great shape has nothing to do with spending a ton
of money.

A lot of people decide to get in shape and immediately rush out and buy an ab belt, a juicer, and a nine-DVD set featuring the stars of *Jersey Shore*. But unless you're already in near-professional-athlete-type shape, all that you really need to do to lose weight and get in shape is move more so you'll burn more calories, take in fewer calories by drinking less soda and eating less fried food, and try to move in a way that works your muscles.

One of my favorite nerdy ways to get in shape is to go to a thrift shop and buy a used VCR. This shouldn't cost more than $10, and you can also probably find a free one on Craigslist or on my street corner once I'm done cleaning the basement. Then buy the corniest vintage workout videos that you can find. There is a fantastic website called VideoFitness.com where you can learn more about which vintage workout videos are the best. A lot of people think this stuff is just for older women, but I have it on good authority from an unreliable source that many professional athletes build their body using Zsa Zsa Gabor's *It's Simple Darling* VHS from 1993 and the *CherFitness: A New Attitude* workout from 1991.

It's a fun, goofy activity, and you can even invite your friends over and have a "Cheesy Workout Night" a few times a week.

Eventually, though, it is entirely possible that your fitness level will surpass the point where Zsa Zsa Gabor, Cher, Nelly, the Teletubbies, and Alyssa Milano can help you. In that case, you just may need to join a gym. But be forewarned! According to a University of California, Berkeley/Stanford study, the average gym member works out just four times per month, so if you're going to pay for a gym membership, make sure you're going to use it.[19]

Here are some tips for signing up for a gym membership without wasting money:

Avoid long-term contracts. Often, gyms will try to get you to agree to a two- or three-year contract, with big penalties for canceling early. Unless you are getting a phenomenal value, stay away from these contracts.

Don't pay for too many months up front. Sometimes gyms will offer big discounts in exchange for paying for many months' worth of dues in advance. This is a sign that the gym is in financial trouble, and is forgoing future cash flows in exchange for large lump-sum payments to cover obligations that are due now. Think about it: Unless you were desperate, why would you take $100 today instead of a deal that would offer you $200 over the next six months? I've talked to people who've bought into these deals only to see the gyms go out of business, and leave them with nothing in exchange for the dues they paid in advance.

Look for ultralow-cost gyms. If there's a YMCA or a Planet Fitness or other budget gym in your area, these can be a fantastic deal if they're clean and not overly skeezy. I once worked out at a cheap gym, until older men tried to show me their genitalia in the locker room, at which point I decided the $9.95 per month I was saving just wasn't worth it. But it's a personal decision that we all have to make for ourselves: At what point do the costs of looking at naked pervs outweigh the savings? This is the kind of cost-benefit analysis calculation that is *the* key to having a good financial life.

I'm Tired of Using Technology

The production of too many useful things results in too many useless people.

—KARL MARX

Some of the most annoying people on the planet (behind the obvious candidates like Ponzi schemers and people with sixteen items in the express lane) are those who are always telling you that they were a fan of something *before everyone else was*.

"Oh, I loved that band back when they were playing little church fund-raisers and elementary school graduations!"

"I had a Facebook account back when it was only available at Harvard! *Did I mention I went to school there?*"

These are the kind of people who will accost you in the supermarket, get right up in your face, and shout, "Oh, you're buying French bread? I was eating French bread before they even had it in America. It wasn't even called French bread back then—it was called *une baguette*!"

Early adopters are really annoying. The good news is they often end up looking like idiots because they overpay for technology that is cheaper and better a couple of years later, or they'll spend a bunch of money and brag about owning something that flops and is obsolete six months later. My favorite example of this is a four-hundred-pound guy who rose to fame for getting the Microsoft Zune logo tattooed on his beached-whale shoulder the month the Zune came out. The brand flopped and was never a serious challenger to the iPod, and this guy will have this tattoo on his shoulder for the rest of his life.[20]

The next person who asks me why I don't have a Kindle or a Nook or a MaxiPad and a Motorola Droid, or any of the other things the kids have today, with their backward hats and their pants around their ankles, and can't live without, is going to walk with a limp for the rest of his or her life.

I'm not anti-technology. I'm anti-stupidity. I'm anti-spending on things you don't need and that won't make your life better. But, if you are considering the purchase of some new technology, here are a few things to keep in mind:

Will this make my life better? Ask yourself: Is this really going to make my day-to-day life better? Or is it just a piece of crap curiosity that you think is kind of cool?

You probably shouldn't buy an e-book reader. Unless you buy a ton of books, you actually don't save any money buying books on Kindles or Nooks or iPads, or whatever. Amazon .com currently offers the latest James Patterson thriller for $12.99 on the Kindle and $15.21 in hardcover—which is also about what you would pay if you bought it at Walmart or Barnes & Noble. When you buy the print version, you can read it in a couple of days and then quickly resell it on Amazon, eBay, or to a local used books store—if those still exist by the time you read this. And, this doesn't even include the cost of the e-reader!

Buying entire CDs is cheaper than buying singles unless it's a brand-new album. I see so many people downloading whole albums on iTunes. This might make sense for brand-new releases but for anything that's more than six months old, check the used listings on Amazon.com first. For instance, let's take the greatest CD in the history of mankind, Duran Duran's *Rio*. It costs $3.96 used on Amazon .com—*including* shipping and handling. It would cost you $13.55 to download the same album, but you don't get the hard disk, cover art, or liner notes. Plus, if you buy CDs, you can still load the songs onto your iPod and then give the CD away as a gift to someone you don't especially care for.

Buy refurbished. Factory-refurbished electronics often come with great warranties and cost a fraction of what buying something brand-new would cost. This can be a great way to buy computers—or TVs, phones, dishwashers, and so on.

Disposable electronics are much, much better. People will often try to sell you more expensive stuff on the grounds that it's "better quality" and "more durable." But most stuff breaks because you drop it, spill something on it, or throw it on the floor really hard because you're in a bad mood. A more expensive laptop is no less susceptible to water damage than a cheap, junky used one. When your electronics are semi-disposable—that is, they don't cost enough for you to freak out too much—your stress level and your credit card balance will be much lower.

When the Phone Doesn't Ring, You'll Know It's Me

The bathtub was invented in 1850 and the telephone in 1875. In other words, if you had been living in 1850, you could have sat in the bathtub for twenty-five years without having to answer the phone.

—BILL DEWITT

Many people suffer from low "cell-esteem"—the pervasive fear that someone, somewhere, has a better cell phone than they do, and is judging them for it and, most likely, having more sex.

Your life will be so much better if you can train yourself to overcome these cell-esteem issues. According to *Consumer Reports*, "The average cell phone user spends about $600 a year on mobile service, while families that talk, text, or use other phone features more than average can spend upward of $1,800."[21]

I'm not here to tell you that you shouldn't have a cell phone; you probably need one. But:

Shop for a cell phone plan online. This is an absolute must for getting a good deal on a cell phone. Walking into a store is a surefire way to overpay. Comparison shop for the best cell phone plans with MyRatePlan.com and PhoneDog.com and with BillShrink.com, which will actually sort through your cell phone bill and then recommend a better plan based on your usage. It's totally free and is something that everyone should try; you will probably save money on your phone bill by using it.

Go with a lesser-known service provider. There are a bunch of companies that basically buy network capacity in bulk from the big boys and then sell it at a discount. Check out plans like Walmart's Straight Talk and MyCricket.com.

Buy a cell phone used and *then* shop for a plan. For most people, buying a cell phone involves snorting a bunch of Adderall, loading some Katy Perry onto your iPod, and then heading off to a mall kiosk to sign up for a free cell phone. The problem is that in order to get something free, you'll have to sign up for a long-term plan. I know what you're thinking: "Wait, wait, wait! Ya mean the cell phone companies aren't offering me a free phone because they care about me? I thought they loved me! They told me they cared!" Sorry kid, love is tough. But if you buy a used cell phone that is 100 percent guaranteed through websites like ReCellular.com or ReplaceYourCell.com, you can then shop around for a discount plan that will have a much lower monthly cost than you'd get at the mall.

Don't buy a cell phone over the phone. If a telemarketer calls and tries to sell you a cell phone, hang up. These deals are generally overpriced at best, and outright scams at worst. And because there's no written contract, it can be unclear what exactly you're agreeing to—and once you activate the phone, you're locked into a long-term commitment. Stay away from these.

Skip the cell phone insurance plan. When you sign up for a cell phone, they will try to sell you an insurance policy for a few dollars per month. As I said in chapter 2, insurance plans like these are usually rip-offs, and if you buy a cell phone cheaply enough, it won't hurt much if you need to replace it.

Text messages. If you're like me, you think the world would be a better place if your interactions with 95 percent of the people you know could be limited to text messages. *sry 4 ur loss :'(* is a much cheaper and environmentally friendly alternative to a condolence card. But CNNMoney recently reported that "[on] a pay-per-text plan, the 160-character messages typically cost 20 cents outgoing and 10 cents incoming. That's a markup of as much as 6,500 percent."[22] In other words, if you could set up a business buying text messages at cost and selling them at the price cell phone companies charge for them, you could start with $15,384.62 and buy text messages and then sell them and become a pre-tax millionaire instantly. If you started this venture with $760 million—ask your parents for a loan for this foolproof venture—you could instantly surpass Warren Buffet's net worth. So sign up for unlimited texting or, if you have a smartphone, use Facebook and e-mail for as much of your communications as you can.

If you think of your cell phone as a status symbol, you will never be financially independent. My cell phone is a Pantech, and I believe the specific model number is "SorryWeWere-TooPoorToBuyYouABlackBerrySoWeGotYouThisInstead." But it works just fine and I actually qualify for a super-cheap data plan because the phone is a piece of crap. People make fun of it, but you can often save a lot of money by buying a cell phone that's a couple of models old.

Smoking

A lot of people say you should quit smoking because it will cause you to die a slow and painful death.

That's garbage, I say. The real reason you should quit smoking is because it is so incredibly freakin' expensive. The difference between great wealth and abject poverty is one or two packs of cigarettes per day. Nationally, the average price of a pack of cigarettes is $5.58. If you smoke two packs per day for fifty years instead of saving that $11.16 per day and investing it, you will miss out on millions! Then there are all the other indirect costs: You smell bad, your teeth look like crap, and life insurance will cost you twice as much if you're a smoker.

Travel

Writing this section is hard for me because I have to confess: I basically hate traveling. I hate staying in hotels, I don't care about eating in exotic restaurants that serve deep-fried monkey testicles, and I like looking at the rain forest in travel magazines much more than I like going into the woods and wearing the same underwear for four weeks and getting malaria. So I'm just wired differently from the large group of people who love to travel, and are willing to go deep into debt to see the world. I admire and in some ways envy your worldly adventurousness. But the fact is, travel is not a necessity; it's a luxury that is most enjoyable when you can actually afford it.

One quick point before some tips: If you want to travel around the world, I'm happy for you. But please, spare me and those around you the existential stories about how your time in Kitschistan changed your whole outlook on life. Travel, learn, experience, enjoy . . . and then shut up about it. And never show anyone your pictures unless he or she asks. We don't care. One of the more popular trends in travel these days is recent grads going abroad for random programs because they graduated and can't find jobs. It's sort of the equivalent of American minor leaguers who go to Japan to play baseball. Except those guys are paid hundreds of millions of yen.

Here are a few ideas for budget travel:

Never, ever, under any circumstances ever, borrow money to go on vacation. "You Work Hard and Deserve a Vacation! Apply Today and Get a Fixed Rate Vacation Loan from CitiFinancial," bellows the ad from Citibank. I've said it before and I'll say it again: If borrowing a bunch of money to get something you hypothetically deserve will put your financial life at risk of collapse—and all the stress that comes with that—it's not worth doing. And since when is there a universal life force that causes people to "deserve" vacations? Unless you have enough cash to go on vacation, and to pay for it without leaving yourself dangerously low on emergency savings, stay home. It's not a no, it's a not yet.

Comparison shop online and look for free deals. Everyone knows to look on sites like Priceline, Travelocity, and Expedia for the best deals on travel. But you can often get a free or very, very steeply discounted vacation by agreeing to listen to a sales pitch for a time-share. Visit sites like VacationPeople .com to find these deals, or e-mail time-share companies. But please, please, please, do not ever let them talk you into buying a time-share. They're generally a terrible deal for consumers and come with all kinds of hidden fees and fine print.

Try bed-and-breakfasts. Staying at a bed-and-breakfast will often be a lot cheaper than staying at a hotel because Bedand Breakfast.com and BBOnline.com have good directories for locations all over the country. Private homes can offer even better deals. My buddy Jason Cochran, a travel writer, once pointed out that hotels in London generally cost upward of $300 per night, but a bedroom in a private home only runs about $33. You could even rent out Virginia Woolf's childhood home for $126 per night. Who's afraid of that?

House swaps! If you have a home in an area that's appealing to vacation-goers (like Somalia, a hot spot for fans of extremely limited government), there are a number of websites that can help you find people with appealing homes of their own to swap with for a week or two. Visit sites like HomeExchange.com, or browse Craigslist.

Try to combine vacationing with career-oriented networking opportunities. Need a vacation? Look into conferences in your field; many of them are in cool destination cities like New York and Las Vegas, and include discounts on hotels. You might even advance your career!

Parking. Studies show that when vacationing, parking is the biggest expense—beating out hotels, transportation, and alcohol—*combined*. Or it can feel that way. Here's my tip for parking: Park in church lots. As long as it's not a Sunday. Whenever I go to Provincetown, I park in the big, spacious lot of a local church—while everyone else pays $453,000 *per hour* for parking. Churches tend to be benevolent places. They're unlikely to tow you. And if you can't find an empty church, type "Sears" into your GPS. I swear, this works in any town. Wherever there's a Sears, there's a large, empty parking lot. It's also a store that's perfectly safe to walk through because you will never be tempted to buy anything.

Get in the Kitchen and Make Me Some Store-Brand Pie That You Bought with Coupons

> When I walk into a grocery store and look at all the products you can choose, I say, "My God!" No king ever had anything like I have in my grocery store today.
>
> —BILL GATES

The title of this section is a *South Park* reference for those of you who are playing along at home. The first rule of saving money on food is to try to throw out less of it. This seems like really obvious, stupid advice, but in 1997, the U.S. Department of Agriculture (USDA) reported that Americans throw out ninety-six billion pounds of food per year: 122 pounds per month for a family of four. Reducing waste by just 5 percent would feed four million people.[23] How do you live with yourself?

The second rule of food is: eat less. No, anorexia is not a good financial strategy. But CNNMoney recently ran a story on a very thin young woman who reported that she had needed to lose weight and save money, so she decided to stop eating dinner. "If I'm really hungry, I'll drink some juice," she said. "Now that I don't have to make dinner, I don't go grocery shopping as often—and when I do, I buy things that can last, like apples, raisins, oatmeal, and soup. So the savings is huge. I used to spend $100 every week and a half, and now it's not more than $30 every two weeks."

Listen up: Skipping dinner and living on $60 per month worth of raisins and oatmeal is not a good financial strategy—or a good digestive health strategy for the comfort of those around you, Paula Abdul.

Which brings us to cooking. The best approach to eating on a budget is to learn to cook well enough to not have to order out, but not so well that you start spending a ton of money on food processors and saffron. I don't know how to cook, I hate cooking, and I don't really want to learn how to cook. All of the culinary talent in my family was soaked up by my cousin Jamie, who was *Food & Wine* magazine's chef of the year (seriously). But I see so many young people who think the solution to the food problem is to just eat cheap crap—and then feel like crap and look like crap.

So, here are some ideas for how to cook when you're horrible at cooking, hate cooking, don't want to spend a bunch of money on food, and want a balanced diet:

Get a rice cooker—but only make brown rice. Rice is really cheap. Brown rice costs only about ten cents per serving—and according to the Food and Drug Administration (FDA), "Diets rich in whole grain foods and other plant foods, and low in total fat, saturated fat, and cholesterol may reduce the risk of heart disease and some cancers." Rice cookers cost less than $30—and make cooking rice easy. You just dump one part rice to two parts water into the cooker, press a button, and then go play online Scrabble for half an hour and when you get back . . . fully cooked rice! Is this a great time to be alive or what?

Memorize the affordable super foods and learn to love them. It's a common complaint that it just costs too much money to eat healthily. That might be true: A 2,000-calorie diet consisting of nothing but store-brand cola and ramen would save you a lot of money. But you'd be so grotesque that you'd never be able to get a job and, even if you could, you'd be too sick to focus. Luckily, a number of very affordable foods are extremely good for you: apples, tofu, black beans, eggs, onions, garbanzo beans (aka chick peas), and popcorn all have important properties that can reduce the risk of everything from heart disease to blindness—just what most of us twentysomethings worry about. And they're not expensive! An excellent book to get started with is *The Complete Idiot's Guide to Eating Well on a Budget.*

Shop farmers' markets late in the day. Just like with yard sales, the best deals at farmers' markets are often found late in the day. If you're not overly picky or looking for really premium stuff, swinging by a weekend farmers' market the hour before it shuts down and everyone goes home can be a really good way to score below-grocery-store prices on fresh, locally grown produce. Plus, it's a slice of Americana. Norman Rockwell would be proud.

Get a slow cooker. A basic Crock-Pot will cost you less than $20 if you get it in a big box store, and as little as $2 if you buy a clean, gently used one at a yard sale. These allow you to throw together a bunch of ingredients in the morning, turn it on, and come home to a warm dinner. If you're too busy to cook, or just hate the idea of coming home from work and messing around in the kitchen for hours, this is a great option. A great slow-cooking cookbook is *Make It Fast, Cook It Slow: The Big Book of Everyday Slow Cooking*, which is the companion to the popular and wonderful blog http://crockpot365 .blogspot.com.

Buying in bulk? If you're young and single, or only live with a roommate or two, buying in bulk at wholesale clubs is probably not going to be worth doing. In addition to the cost of the membership, there's the time and money you'll spend driving there—and all the food you'll throw out when you discover that a 144-pack of hot dog buns isn't the way to go. But stocking up on nonperishables when they're on sale at the grocery store and you have coupons? Totally worth doing. Buy baked beans and toilet paper in bulk—synergy!

If you believe in eating organic, recognize that it's less important for some foods. The Environmental Working Group lists these foods as having the lowest pesticide residues: papayas, broccoli, cabbage, bananas, kiwifruit, sweet peas (frozen), asparagus, mangoes, pineapple, sweet corn (frozen), avocados, and onions.[24] So don't bother buying those organic.

Use a grocery list. A study published in the *International Journal of Retail & Distribution Management*—I know, my favorite bathroom reading, too—reports that "the findings are conclusive: written shopping lists significantly reduce average expenditure."[25] Like so many other things, having a plan is a key to winning. This doesn't need to be fancy, but making a list of the things you need before you go into the store can help you avoid buying stuff you don't really want.

Consider buying groceries online. One of the richest people I know buys Crystal Light in bulk on Amazon.com. With free super-saver shipping on orders more than $25—some items are excluded—this can be cheaper than the grocery store depending on where you live. And, if you "Subscribe to Post Shredded Wheat," you can save an extra 15 percent; you just set up a regular plan to have it delivered. No muss, no fuss, and you won't be tempted to buy something else while you're in the store. One study found that Internet food shopping leads to fewer impulse purchases than shopping at brick-and-mortar stores.[26]

Drink vegetable juice! The hardest-hitting piece of journalism I've ever done concerned V8. They were labeling their six packs as "weekly packs" with a serving of vegetables for every day of the week—an odd choice given that a week has either five or seven days depending on how you look at it, but certainly not six. In any case: Only about 11 percent of Americans meet the USDA guidelines for fruit and vegetable servings per day—and reduced-sodium vegetable juice is a convenient, affordable way of getting more into your diet.[27]

Buy coupons online! Cutting coupons out of the Sunday newspaper is the classic way to save money on groceries. The problem is that you probably don't buy the newspaper on Sunday anyway (mainly because you're under the age of 106), so you'd have to buy a copy specifically for the purpose of getting the coupons—which might result in breaking even at best and, perhaps, buying a bunch of stuff you might not really like just because of the coupons. But the Internet has led to an awesome new trend in couponing that allows you to search for just the coupons you want in quantities that, if you bought the number of newspapers you'd need to get that many coupons, would put you in the Hoarders Hall of Fame. TheCoupon Clippers.com offers thousands of different coupons for, on average, about 10 percent of the savings you'll get on the item (not including doubling). You can order many copies of each coupon so, if you have a few items you like to buy regularly, this can save you a *ton* of money.

Get coupons from friends. CBS MoneyWatch offers this advice: "Do ask friends and neighbors to leave aside papers. Some people actually subscribe to newspapers for the articles, not the coupons. It's perfectly acceptable to ask these friends and family members— politely—to set aside the coupons for you to pick up at a later time." My favorite thing about this tip is the completely unnecessary admonition to be polite when you're asking people to save the coupon section of their local newspaper. Seriously though, this is important. "Hey,

@#$@##$%! Give me the coupons for the Oreos; you're fat enough as it is!" is not a good way to score free coupons or stay on good terms with your grandmother.

Stock up when stuff's on sale. Over the past twenty years, food prices have increased, on average, 2.5 percent per year—and many experts expect that the rate of inflation in food prices will be higher in the near future. With savings accounts paying less than 1 percent in interest, there's an argument to be made for putting a good chunk of your savings in canned beans in your garage, or under your bed. Buy shaving cream and all the rest when it's on sale—and you'll beat inflation, never run out, and never pay full price.[28]

Restaurants

It is entirely possible to earn $40,000 per year pretax, rent an apartment for $1,000 per month, and then spend the rest of it eating meals at lower-end national chain restaurants. You will end up fat, broke, and single.

I'm not opposed to the idea of eating at restaurants, especially if you're smart about it and keep an eye on how much you're spending. Here are some of my tips:

> **Be wary of restaurants that don't place a dollar sign on the menu.** Researchers at the Center for Hospitality Research at Cornell University found that, on average, people will spend more money when ordering off menus that price items at "15" instead of "$15." The researchers suggest that taking the dreaded $ symbol off the menu eliminates the "pain of paying."[29]
>
> **Coupons.** We—yes, you and me—are in the Golden Age of Coupons for American Restaurants. There's Groupon.com, Restaurant.com, ValPak.com, and various smartphone apps.

Ask to have half your order boxed up before it arrives. This one comes from my friend Ramit Sethi and it's brilliant. Portions in restaurants are huge, but if they bring it out you'll probably eat all of it and end up looking like Eric Cartman. Box it up early before you're tempted and you'll end up with something for lunch, a fatter wallet, and a thinner waistline. **Plan ahead.** A big part of keeping restaurant costs down is planning ahead: You can't just show up for dinner and hope that the other person will pick up the check; you have to plan strategically to make sure that the other person gets stuck with the check. My advice? Arrange to get a very important phone call late in the meal—or, you can simply excuse yourself to go to the restroom a few minutes before the check arrives. Chances are your dining companion will pay while you're away. Just kidding. Don't really do this. At least, not more than once. But it is worth keeping track of which restaurants have special deals on what nights.

Buying Used: Save Yourself, Save the Planet

Second hand curls
I'm wearing second hand pearls;
I never get a single thing that's new
Even Jake the Plummer, he's the man I adore
Had the nerve to tell me he's been married before!

—FROM THE SONG "SECOND HAND ROSE," ORIGINALLY SUNG BY FANNY BRICE AND LATER BY BARBRA STREISAND. YOUTUBE IT RIGHT NOW!

The single greatest thing you can do to save the planet (other than buying nothing) is to buy stuff used. Seriously, a used fur coat is better for the environment than a new organic hemp skirt.

It also happens to be one of the most powerful ways to improve your financial life.

It's also, if you get into it, really freakin' fun.

My mother—the self-proclaimed Yard Sale Queen of North Falmouth, Massachusetts—was the master of this. She and I went yard-sale-ing every single weekend from the time I was four until . . . well, now, as a matter of fact, whenever we're together.

We couldn't get my brother or my dad interested in joining us, but for most of my childhood, nearly all of my clothing, toys, and books were purchased at yard sales for about ten cents on the dollar— five cents on the dollar if I did the haggling because six-year-olds drive a hard bargain ("Excoooze me siwwww; awl I have is my two dowwar awwowance; will you take that for this vintage xylophone you have pwiced at four?").

Then I got home and listed it on eBay. Just kidding. Sometimes I actually bought stuff because I wanted it.

When you grow up shopping that way, everything in stores seems that much more expensive and you really do think twice about parting with money. Here are a couple of other things I learned from shopping at yard sales:

Most stuff that people buy that they think they will love ends up being sold new—or barely used—at a yard sale. Do this experiment: Go on Craigslist next Friday night and find some yard sales in your area. Make a list, and then spend Saturday morning going to the sales and looking at all the crap people paid $20 for that they are now trying to sell for $2. Then next time you're in a store and you're debating whether to buy something, visualize those yard sales. How much of the stuff you're buying today will end up there in a few years?

You always have to check prices. Yard sales are one of the least efficient marketplaces in the world. You always have to check prices because it is entirely possible to see the same book at three different yard sales on the same day priced anywhere from ten cents to $3. When you shop at yard sales, you become conditioned to always be aware of how much something costs, which makes you a savvy consumer no matter where you're shopping.

Plus, there's the environmental aspect of yard sales. No matter how eco-friendly the method of production is, manufacturing always uses resources. Cash for Clunkers is, perhaps, the best example of this. Proponents of the program claimed that by getting old gas guzzlers off the road and replacing them with new, smaller, more fuel-efficient vehicles, it would help the environment.

Except that it didn't. Once you took into account the huge amount of environmental resources used in manufacturing the old cars, the program was closer to being an environmental wash—and an expensive one at that.[30]

Then there are the financial benefits. In his awesome book *The Cheapskate Next Door*, Jeff Yeager surveyed the shopping practices of some of the best consumers in America. He reports that "When cheapskates shop for things they need, they're ideally looking to buy things that will increase in value. Second best is buying something that will retain its value."

The masters of this, according to Yeager, are the Amish. "The Amish are known for aggressively buying up antiques at estate auctions and other public sales," he writes. "To my surprise, their passion for owning antiques seemed less a matter of personal taste . . . than it was a matter of wanting to own something that would likely retain its value or even appreciate in value."[31]

When you look at the total cost of ownership—that is, the impact a purchase has on your net worth over the long term—buying used just makes so much more sense than buying new.

This is why I hate IKEA. To pay $79.99 for a particleboard dresser that you can assemble at home might seem like a good idea, but as soon as you put it together, it's absolutely worthless. According to the Antique Collectors' Club in England's *Antique Furniture Price Index*, furniture outperformed both the stock market and the housing market from the index's inception through the year 2000.[32]

This is not to say that you should pour all of your money into antique furniture, but if you're going to have furniture in your house—which you must—you might as well buy something that won't lose value and might even go up in value. The other advantage to buying used is that it takes time—which means that, if you enjoy shopping, it's more cost-effective than heading to Walmart with your American Express card and an envelope of crushed up Adderall. In her *Housewives' Guide to Antiques*, published in 1959, Leslie Gross helpfully explained that "specific antique items are not always found at the first door, and may require some enjoyable searching for just the exact article you desire . . . this is one way to get in a lot of shopping with a little buying."

For furnishing your place, flea markets and yard sales are a must. Although there are bargains in every category, furniture usually represents the best deal—selling for at least 90 percent off of retail. This is because the seller has to find a buyer who has a place for it—which is much harder to do with a couch than it is with, say, a handbag or a used book. Furnishing your home the vintage way is actually cheaper than going to IKEA or Walmart. Leslie Gross had it right when she wrote that "as long as you must have furniture anyway, you might as well have beautiful furniture. It costs no more, yet gives infinitely more pleasure."

This was how I furnished the condo I bought to live in during college; and it's now rented out, fully furnished, for a significant premium to what other units in the area rent for because of the quality of the decor. I found a vintage black leather chair for $5, along with a $10 glass end table. My contemporary dining room set cost $60, including delivery, and the Art Deco flamingo mirror I bought for $5 regularly sells on eBay for $90. The first piece I bought for the

condo, a custom-framed exhibition poster for an Erte's gallery opening in New York City cost just $15, after I haggled down from a $45
asking price. It sells on eBay for $100+, unframed, but it still hangs
on my wall as I write this.

Furnishing your home with flea market finds allows it to truly
become your home. "When you shop at a flea market you are on your
own, without the reassurance that comes with the advertised, mass-
produced purchase, accompanied by an illustration on the package
showing you how to use it and where to put it," says Rachel Ashwell,
founder of Shabby Chic. "At the flea market, your own taste is your
only guide—uninfluenced by what is currently being pushed in the
shop windows and mail-order catalogs. Here you can express yourself
in how you furnish your home, the clothes you wear, or the presents
you give."[33]

I can think of no better argument for the psychological benefits
of buying used; it's the last bastion of individuality. Plus, the stories of
your finds will be so much more interesting than someone who went
into Walmart with a credit card and bought all the particleboard
bookcases he could fit in one cart. It's just as Christian Dior once said:
"I don't want anything new. It has to have a well-worn feel to it, old
and rich in memories."[34]

Here are some tips for furnishing your place at auctions, yard
sales, and flea markets:

Know when to go. Use Craigslist and your local newspaper's
Friday edition to find yard sales, and then show up early to
get the best stuff (this is when antique dealers go) and go
early to mid-afternoon to score deals on stuff that wasn't
snapped up early. Often, furniture doesn't sell quickly at
yard sales—because it's painful to move and because it really
needs the right buyer, whereas a nice piece of china will sell
to anyone who appreciates quality—so the afternoon can be
a fantastic time to score deals on furniture.

Use AuctionZip.com to find auctions in your area. If you've never been to one, you should go just to see what it's like. And don't think that auctions are all about stuffy New Yorkers wagging their pinkies and using phrases like "post-modernist," "deconstructionist," and "magical realism," paying millions for paintings of rectangles. Most auction houses are in smaller towns where stuff sells for anywhere from five dollars to a few hundred. Auctions can be a fantastic way to get stuff like couches, beds, and dining room tables for a tiny fraction of what you'd pay at an antiques store or even at a flea market. Plus, if the auctioneer is good, they're really fun.

Be open-minded and flexible. When you go into a retail store, having a shopping list is the key to avoiding impulse buying and overspending. But at a flea market, finding something you didn't know you needed until the second you saw it is where the fun is. And you will drive yourself nuts if you wander from yard sale to yard sale looking for a certain chair you saw in a catalog. Develop your own style as you shop, and be open to whatever grabs your attention.

Try used or vintage gifting. A poll conducted by the Center for a New American Dream found that 39 percent of Americans "would welcome lower holiday spending and less emphasis on gift giving a lot." Finding something at a thrift shop that really reminds you of a friend emphasizes your bond much more than a $25 gift card to Abercrombie & Fitch. In her book *Money Secrets of the Amish*, Lorilee Craker describes how the Amish divide up gifting as a matter of tradition: "Most Amish families pick names out of a hat and buy one Christmas gift for one family member each year." That's right, tell your circle of friends that it's time to go Amish.

Buy refurbished computers on eBay. I do. You can get a good laptop for $200–$300 from a PowerSeller (someone with a long-established track record of delivering quality service), often loaded with software. Another benefit? You're saving the planet. The manufacture of a laptop produces 4,000 times that laptop's weight in industrial waste. This comes in especially handy for me because I regularly invent new ways to break laptops. In the past two years alone, I've broken laptops by spilling tea on one and by dropping another on my foot. Knowing that the laptop only cost a couple hundred dollars reduced the pain.

You absolutely must haggle. Sometimes a simple "What's your best price on this?" will work wonders. Another trick? Just stare at an item, pick it up, put it down, inspect it—and let the dealer talk him- or herself down.

Charity

We make a living by what we get, we make a life by what we give.

—ATTRIBUTED TO WINSTON CHURCHILL

If your goal is to be happy, charity is important. Studies out of Harvard and the University of British Columbia found that donating money actually produces a greater happiness boost than spending money.[35]

My mother once gave a handle of vodka to a homeless guy. She had it in her car, saw him on the side of the road, and impulsively pulled over. His eyes lit up with excitement and appreciation. This goes to show that just because you come at something with a generous spirit does not mean you're going to do any good.

Here are some possibly better, or at least lower-proof, ideas for how you can make the most out of your charitable giving:

Donate monthly. Just as funding your retirement accounts automatically is a good way to save for the future without having to think about it, most major charities will let you set up a monthly automated withdrawal from your account— with as little as $5. You won't even notice the difference, but it will add up and you'll feel like a better person.

Check out the charity before you donate. Before you send money, investigate the charity a little to make sure that your donations aren't just being used to finance excessive salaries for executives. Check out CharityNavigator.org for ratings of charities based on their effectiveness and frugality, that is, the percentage of their donations that are used for helping people rather than administrative expenses.

Bigger charities have scale; your donation will go further. It can be tempting to help upstart charities and I'm not saying you shouldn't. But big charities that handle lots of money often have better infrastructure and are more efficient in terms of getting the money where it needs to go. In the wake of the earthquake in Haiti for instance, millions of people pulled out their cell phones to donate money to Wyclef Jean's charity Yéle. But as Felix Salmon reported, "Yéle is not the soundest of charitable institutions: It has managed only one tax filing in its twelve-year existence, and it has a suspicious habit of spending hundreds of thousands of dollars on paying either Wyclef Jean personally or paying companies where he's a controlling shareholder, or paying his recording-studio expenses."[36] I don't mean to say that Wyclef is a bad guy but when you have multiple options for supporting the same goal (e.g., natural disaster relief), go with large, established charities with international reputations.

Practice random acts of kindness. Improving the lives of others doesn't have to be about grand acts of charity. In her book *All the Money in the World*, Laura Vanderkam suggests paying the toll of the car behind you on the highway as a way of spreading a bit of happiness. I love this idea, but don't blame me if it leads to confusion at the toll booth, delaying traffic; or the car behind you, assuming something you did not intend, follows you home for a shag. Come to think of it, maybe stick with more purposeful, if still random, acts of kindness. Like sandwiches—not vodka—for homeless people.

Financial Help from Parents

Many young people will have the awkwardly good fortune of having their parents offer to help them with financial issues: everything from paying off student loans to providing the down payment for a house to paying for a car. I have some friends in their thirties with stable jobs whose parents just feel a compulsion to send them money whenever possible.

Some people just don't feel comfortable with this. Get over it— and feel free to blame me, your financial advisor: Never turn down free money, whether from a 401(k) employer match or from parents bursting with love and resources. Here are some general principles for parental help with money:

> **There is nothing wrong with living with your parents.** Really. If you live near your parents anyway and are trying to get out of debt and build savings, cutting your living expenses for a while can be a real financial game changer. According to one survey, 85 percent of recent grads moved back in with their parents at least for a little while;[37] it's nothing to be ashamed of. **But don't accept "help" with a down payment on a car.** I have one friend whose dad gave him the down payment for a $28,000 car with high monthly payments. I know his dad meant well, but what he really should have done is offered

the kid cash to pay for a used car. A gift that leads to a bunch of debt and an asset guaranteed to depreciate is not helpful; it's like giving someone rope.

If your parents want to help, ask for help paying off student loans. One of the best ways for your parents to help is with your student loans. By getting rid of your debt, they'll be helping you come up with cash to save for retirement or buy a house—and decreasing the stress in your life and lowering the amount of interest you'll pay.

CHAPTER 6

Here in My (Paid For) Car, I Feel Safest of All

If you think nobody cares if you're alive, try missing a couple of car payments.

—EARL WILSON

This chapter assumes that you actually need a car, or it is at least advantageous for you to have one. I'm assuming you can figure out on your own whether you need a car and are, of course, aware of public transportation and options like Zipcar for people who only need cars sporadically. You can save thousands of dollars per year by goin' pedestrian. For an excellent primer on how to do this, check out Chris Balish's book *How to Live Well Without Owning a Car.*

Lou Pizarro is an ex-marine who weighs about three hundred pounds and will hunt you down if you don't pay your car bill. He's been pepper sprayed, run over—even shot at—and it's all part of the excitement. He loves his work and seems like a good guy, but I'm pretty sure you don't want to meet him; he's a repo man.

He has a pretty good firsthand view of the stupidity that people get themselves into with cars.

"It's really kind of crazy what people do for their cars," he writes. "I guess it's a psychological thing: You want to keep up with the

Joneses and impress the ladies. People buy all kinds of fancy speakers and rims for their car—I've seen cars with 15-, 20,000-dollar sound systems on them—then they don't make payments on the car itself![1]

"You gotta do your part," Pizzaro advises. "You gotta be responsible and make your payments. Then you're never gonna see us."

The problem is that the only way you can really guarantee that you'll never have your car repossessed is to not have car payments. Think about it: As long as you have a monthly car payment, your ability not to have Mr. Pizarro show up in your driveway with pepper spray and a tow truck is dependent at least in part on factors beyond your control. If you lose your job or get sick, you simply might not be able to make your payments.

Wouldn't life be less stressful without having to worry about the possibility of three-hundred-pound Lou showing up at your house in the middle of the night? This is not hypothetical: According to *Automotive News*, 1.5 million cars were repossessed in 2010.

There are very few mentalities that can torpedo your financial life to the extent that the wrong attitude about buying cars can. The average American driver spends $9,641 per year on car-related expenses.[2] If Americans funneled the money they spend on cars into paying off the national debt, we would have the entire debt paid off in less than a decade. If we cut our driving costs and funnel that money into achieving financial security instead, we'd all end up rich—instead of just looking rich.

But it's hard. Because the people marketing cars sell you on the exact opposite idea. One car ad promoted a luxury car as a way to "reduce stress."[3] The problem is that there is not one iota of evidence that driving a nicer car makes you less stressed in any way at all.

Actually, the need to generate the income to afford those payments—possibly by working more hours than you want to at a job you hate—is what creates stress. The reality is literally the exact opposite of what they're saying. Marketers lie. Who knew?

People can be really irrational when it comes to buying cars.

Suze Orman writes that she sees so many Americans "shelling out big bucks for tricked-out cars you can't afford because of some insane need to impress people you don't even know who pull up alongside you at red lights."

Here's the thing: Most people are too busy battling their own insecurities to bother judging you about yours. That's what my mother told me about my insecurities when I was elementary school, and ya know what? When I talk to people from back then now, she was 100 percent right. So, everyone goes into debt trying to put on a show to impress other people who are also going into debt to do the same thing—and everyone's miserable from going into debt, and also too busy to bother judging.

That's *stupid*.

Let's look at the math:

According to Edmunds.com, the average monthly payment on a new car is $479.[4]

If you spend $479 per month on car payments from the age of twenty-one to the age of sixty-five, you will end up having shelled out $252,912. But if you invested that $479 per month at an average annual return of 10 percent, you would end up with $4,126,517. If that new-car smell is worth $4.1 million to you, I don't know what to say. And, by the way, there's some evidence that that new-car smell is seriously toxic and possibly dangerous. One Japanese study found that the volatile organic chemicals in a fresh-out-of-the-factory mini-van were thirty-five times the healthy limit and could cause head-aches, dizziness, and respiratory problems. The *Daily Telegraph* compared the new-car smell to glue sniffing.[5] The difference is that glue sniffing is an affordable pastime. Note from lawyer: Don't sniff glue.

The difference between living on a steady diet of government cheese and accumulating more wealth than less than 1 percent of American households is all in the car you drive. Something to think about, perhaps, the next time you're watching car commercials.

So why do people shell out money they don't have for expensive cars? To find the answer, I conducted the most rigorous method of scientific research I know how to do: I asked my friends on Facebook.

What followed was a string of thirty-one comments from my pro new-car friends explaining their rationale for their purchases, and me taking the tone of condescending moderator with the help of a few snarky used-car drivers who piled on.

My favorite pro new-car comment: "[The car you drive does] have an impact on how you feel about yourself."

If you need an expensive car that will make you poor to feel good about yourself, you don't need a car. You need a therapist. It's one of the reasons that, according to research by Dr. Thomas J. Stanley, the overwhelming majority of self-made millionaires cite high self-esteem as a major contributor to their ability to build net worth. Yet people do identify with their cars. One survey found that nearly *half of car owners view their cars as a reflection of who they are.*[6] Seriously, get a life.

If a mass-produced piece of steel that causes global warming and kills people when it crashes into them reflects your idealized self, I'm not really sure what to say. If you don't have a strong sense of self, you're unlikely to be good with money. It's hard to take care of your own financial interests when you're trying to prop up your own ego with cash.

And the worst part is that it doesn't even work. Dr. Stanley reports that "there is no significant correlation between the make [brand] of motor vehicle you drive and your level of happiness with life."

A study published in the *Journal of Consumer Psychology* found that the act of driving is not any more enjoyable in a nicer car after just a few weeks of ownership.

"Once we have owned the car for a few weeks, it no longer captures all of our attention, and other things will be on our minds while driving," explains the fabulously named Norbert Schwarz, a marketing professor at the University of Michigan. "As soon as that happens, we would feel just as well driving a cheaper alternative."[7]

This is, by the way, one of the dangers of test-driving a bunch of different cars. Because you'll be focused on the joy and feel of the car you're driving, it will seem much more important. But once you own a car, it won't.

It's also the reason rich people actually don't usually buy expensive cars. Remember Dr. Stanley's research: Two out of three buyers or leaseholders of brand-new foreign-made luxury cars are not millionaires.[8] The most popular car make among millionaires? Toyota.[9] That's right: Most drivers of luxury cars aren't rich, and most rich people don't drive luxury cars.

Dr. Stanley also found that net worth accounts for only 10.5 percent of the factors that determine how much money a person will spend on a car. Dr. Stanley writes on his blog that "More than 80 percent of the variation in purchase price is unaccounted for by either wealth or income. In other words, you wouldn't want to bet the farm that the fellow sitting next to you in church who drives an expensive car is a millionaire. And the proportion of explained variance is considerably less among those who lease their vehicles."[10]

So if you want to look like a millionaire, you should buy a used Toyota. Actually, if you want to drive like a millionaire, you should drive whatever car you can afford to pay for with cash. That's the one common theme among cars driven by millionaires.

Car Leases Should Come with an "I Am a Moron" Bumper Sticker

Before we get into the nitty-gritty of how to buy a car, this needs to be said: If you lease a car, you're an idiot. If anyone you know leases a car, he or she is an idiot.

For the uninitiated, a car lease is basically a long-term car rental agreement. The difference is that if it was actually called a rental, people would say "What? I'm going to rent a car for two years?

That's stupid." So instead, car dealers call it a lease. To lease a car, you put down some money up front (usually a few thousand dollars) and then pay to use the car each month, but you don't own it. Because you are renting, the monthly payments tend to look lower than if you were buying the car. This is why people lease cars: "More car for less money! Wahoo!"

This line of thinking will drive you right into the poorhouse. The *Consumer Reports* Money Lab ran the numbers on leasing versus buying and concluded that buying a 2008 Honda Accord EX new for $24,495 "would cost $4,597 less over five years than closed-end leasing for exactly the same model."[11] That doesn't even take into account the buildup in equity in the purchased car! It also doesn't factor in the other problem with leasing: Since you are driving something that isn't yours, the dealer will nail you to a cross if you do anything to damage it. And sometimes you don't even need to damage it. Data from marketing research firm CNW shows that 35 percent of lease-holders end up exceeding the mileage limits—and are forced to pay, on average, an extra $1,700 to the dealer to make up for it. This is a really crappy way to try to get ahead financially.

People who lease cars don't get rich. This is why, according to Dr. Thomas J. Stanley, most self-made millionaires have never leased a car in their entire life, including before they were rich. So don't lease a car. Ever.

New Cars Aren't Much Better

According to Dave Ramsey you should never buy a new car unless you have a net worth of a million dollars.

That sounds hyper-conservative but he has a good point. Unless you're already financially independent, you really can't afford the immediate, guaranteed loss that comes with buying a new car. New cars lose, on average, about 20 percent of their value the second you drive them off the lot[12]—and lose about half their value within four years.

If you buy a new car for $30,000 once every four years and then trade it in for a new one, you end up losing $3,750 per year from depreciation on your car alone. That's about 10 percent of the median per capita income in America evaporating over your shoulder. And that doesn't include any of the other expenses associated with driving a car. Can you afford this? Most people can't. Buy a used car instead.

Think of it this way: In four years, your Mercedes will be a Prius. Allow me to illustrate.

At this writing, a new 2010 Toyota Prius II was listed on Cars .com for $23,750. (This is the entry-level model.)

On the same site, a 2006 Mercedes-Benz M-Class ML350 4MATIC with 60,745 miles on it was listed for $23,988.

The point is, turning something that costs more than most people make in a year into something worth less than half its original price in a span of four years is not a good financial plan.

"But wait!" you exclaim. "Couldn't the savings of buying a car new and taking really good care of it and not having to worry about repairs outweigh the savings of buying used cars?"

Yes, it could. And I could be Justin Bieber. But I'm not, and you won't save money by buying a new car. Stick with used cars until you're really rich. And even then, you will probably be just as happy if you stick with used cars.

A Word About Hybrids

Unless you commute from California to Maine daily, the cost of buying a brand-new hybrid—especially the immediate hit that you'll take in depreciation when you drive it off the lot—will outweigh the savings on gas compared with paying cash for an older used car.

In a few years, when you can buy a reliable five- or seven-year-old hybrid for a few thousand bucks, that will change. For now, unless you have a ton of cash, skip the hybrids.

No Car Payments? That's Crazy Talk!

If following the conventional wisdom were the way to do well financially, most people would be doing well financially. But actually, most people are doing horribly financially. I am part of a tiny, fringe cult of people who think we should only buy cars with cash. That's right: no loans. But what's interesting is that every single person I've ever met who agrees with me on this is rich.

My grandfather used to tell a story—over and over—about the time he went to a Florida car dealership to buy a new Infiniti. When the dealer asked him how he wanted to finance it, he replied that he would write a check.

"What are you, Mafia? Only drug dealers pay cash for cars!" said the incredulous dealer.

My grandfather got up and left without a word.

The problem with buying cars exclusively with cash is that it's probably not going to get you the nicest car right off the bat. At all. If you can manage to buy something that doesn't elicit ridicule from at least 80 percent of your friends, you're doing well. But when you don't have a car payment, it actually becomes pretty easy to save up the cash to buy a new (used) car.

Here's the math: You start out by scraping together $1,300 in cash to buy a piece-of-crap car. Let's say it's the 2001 Kia Optima SE I found on Craigslist. According to the ad, it has all the options— leather seats, sunroof, alloy wheels, and a few dents—but it's "reliable cheap transportation."

Instead of ponying up and buying yourself a brand-new car, you drive that piece of crap for two years, while automatically diverting the $479 per month you would have been using for payments on a new car into a special savings account you have cleverly labeled "NotAPieceOfCrapKiaCarFund."

At the end of two years, you have $11,496 in that fund. Plus you sell the Kia for, let's say, $900. By the way, the really cool thing about buying old crappy cars is that they basically don't go down in value.

A perfect example of this is my friend Ellen who, believe it or not, once bought a 1989 Buick Century from her neighbor's son for $200. She drove it for a year and then sold it on Craigslist for $425 to "some mom who needed a back middle seat belt." The only repair she had to make? New windshield wipers.

This is more common than you'd think because stuff that's old and crappy really doesn't have any intrinsic value, so it's worth whatever you can negotiate for it. If you have a good eye for a bargain and know how to negotiate, you can probably make money on your crap cars.

Anyway—now you have $12,396 that you can use to buy a less crappy car. This time, you get a 2007 Honda Accord.

Drive that for three years and keep saving that $479 per month car payment and . . . you get the picture.

And we're not even including the interest you'll earn on the money saved while you wait to buy the car.

If you *decided* to keep driving less-than-impressive cars, you could divert that money toward a down payment on a house, which, as you'll learn in the next chapter, is a key part of building a strong financial future, recent headlines notwithstanding.

And never have a car payment for the rest of your life.

And never have to deal with the stress of a high monthly payment that can make the most stressful times—illness, job loss, getting dumped, and so on—infinitely more stressful.

How to Buy a Car You Can Actually Afford

Buying a cheap used car is not without its risks. I can just hear half of the people reading this screaming, "But it'll break down! I'll be stranded on the side of the road! It's not safe!"

My advice? Talk to Irv Gordon and then shut up. In 1966, Irv

Gordon bought a Volvo, and he's driven it ever since. It has 2.6 million miles on it. So if you think your 2002 Honda is in need of an upgrade, shut up. *Wired* asked Gordon if he thought it would ever get to the point where the car just won't start and he has to replace it.

His response was classic: "No such thing, it'd never happen. If it didn't start, I'd find out why it didn't start and fix it."[13]

The bias against buying used cars dates back to a time when cars were much less reliable than they are today (think of those sold by Matilda's father, if you saw that movie or read the book). Over the past few decades, there has been an unbelievable improvement in the reliability and durability of automobiles. In 2001, *Consumer Reports* reported that "back in 1980, the average trouble rate for all new vehicles was 88 problems reported for every 100 cars. By 2000 that rate had dropped to 20 problems: an astounding 77 percent improvement."[14]

It's simply a lot more possible to find a reliable used car than it used to be. Of course, you can still get burned badly if you're not careful. Here are some tips for buying a used car:

You only need about $1,000. Philip Reed, the senior consumer advice editor for Edmunds.com, says that $1,000–$1,500 is all it takes to get a reliable car these days. Many of the popular concerns about it being impossible to find reliable cars in that price range are outdated, he says. "When I was growing up in the '70s, the expectation was that a car would go for about 100,000 miles and then you were living on borrowed time," he says. "But I've bought cars that had 110,000 and driven them for 60,000 more. There's a lot of people still believing that 100,000 miles is a ton of miles but it's not."

Find a way to come up with the $1,000 or so it takes to get a first car. Please, spare me the "I can't possibly scrape together $1,000 to buy a used car! I just have to borrow $20,000 to buy a new one." And, if you can't put your hands on $1,000, that's all the more reason you can't afford to sign up for car payments.

Check with friends and family first. A lot of people have old cars they're looking to get rid of and, buying from someone you know, you can usually get a good deal. Plus, you'll have a better idea of the history of the car. Granny's not gonna sell you a lemon because you know where she lives.

Don't buy a used car without having a mechanic look at it first. Maybe you have a friend or relative who can do this for free. If not, it will cost less than $100 and you'll learn whether there are any major red flags. Jacob Joseph, a mechanic and editor with CarBuzz.com, notes that the mechanic will also be able to tell you which problems would need to be taken care of immediately—and which ones you can put off for a while.

Research the history. Joseph also suggests getting a vehicle history report. "This will show any accidents it may have been involved with and what (if any) damage may have occurred," he says. "A car history report should come from the owners and you then compare it against any possible recalls or technical service bulletins (TSBs). By law, all information about recalls and manufacturer repairs must be free of charge. In addition, any proper dealership will have this information on file." Reed suggests signing up for one month of access to Carfax.com—which runs about $30—if you're in the market for a car, but adds that many websites also offer free access to the vehicle history report with their car listings.

Stick with a common car. High-performance cars are cool (and hot—go figure), but also tend to need a lot of repairs, and the parts can be expensive. *Consumer Reports* found that "Quality and reliability are not the same thing. . . . Small cars are the most reliable car type as a group, and luxury cars, especially luxury SUVs, are the most troublesome."[15]

So while you're in the "Pay-cash-for-crappy-cars-so-in-a-few-years-I-can-pay-cash-for-a-nice-car" stage of life, buy something more average. Edmunds.com calls the 2003 Hyundai Elantra a "2010 Used Car Best Bet"—and you can get one for less than $4,000. Great gas mileage, too![16]

The bottom line is this: Even though it's a lot easier to sign up for a loan to buy a really cool new car, it will prevent you from ever getting ahead financially. Socking away the money that would have gone to car payments will afford you a lifetime of never having car payments. According to LendingTree, this is a stage of financial freedom that an astounding 70 percent of Americans haven't reached[17]—and you have a chance to reach it right now.

As an added bonus, you'll never meet Lou Pizarro.

CHAPTER 7

A Place for Your Stuff

In the song "Tea for Two," the hero laments that he is "discontented with homes that are rented." It comes from the Broadway musical *No, No, Nanette*, which, legend has it, Red Sox owner and budding theater producer Harry Frazee financed by selling Babe Ruth to the New York Yankees in 1920—and marking something approximating the beginning of an eighty-six-year World Series drought for the Boston Red Sox.

No, No, Nanette is of course long forgotten, and Babe Ruth became arguably the greatest player in the history of baseball. So the sale was, to put it mildly, one of the worst investment decisions ever made.

But at the time, maybe it made sense. Ruth was coming off one of the worst seasons of his career as a pitcher, and while he was making the transition into a great power hitter, he hadn't yet put up anything close to the numbers that would come as a member of the Yankees.

The point is this: Be a contrarian. Whether it's baseball players or houses, the best time to buy is often when everyone else is pessimistic.

On September 6, 2010, *Time* magazine's cover story was "Rethinking Homeownership: Why Owning a Home May No Longer Make Economic Sense."

The headline was eerily similar to a *BusinessWeek* cover story from August 1979 that bore the headline "The Death of Equities." That story followed a rout in the market similar to the one that hit again thirty years later and noted that "the death of equities looks like an almost permanent condition—reversible someday, but not soon."[1]

That story landed—almost to the day—at the bottom of the market and marked the beginning of a stock market run-up that lasted twenty years and was the longest and biggest bull market in U.S. history.

My point is not to rag on *BusinessWeek* or *Time* (although it sure is fun) but to show that the best investments have been made at times when everyone thinks they're stupid. A recent poll from the National Foundation for Credit Counseling found that about half of Americans no longer think that homeownership is a realistic way of building wealth.[2]

The irony is that the drop in home prices makes homeownership a more realistic way of building wealth than it was when home prices were inflated. As real estate mogul Matthew A. Martinez notes in his book *How to Make Money in Real Estate in the New Economy*, "Always remember that there are just as many, if not more, profitable opportunities to pursue during the doom and gloom years associated with a bust as there are during the go-go days associated with the boom."

Investments are the only field where people see stuff go on sale and conclude that that makes it a bad time to buy. What would you call someone who refused to buy canned goods because they were on sale? An idiot. It's the same with investments.

You'll probably never get rich if you rent your home. Hypothetically, it's possible. But for the most part, in America, the path to wealth has included homeownership. And I doubt that a couple of years of falling home prices following an unprecedented run-up in home prices negates hundreds of years of history.

According to the Federal Reserve Board, the median net worth of a homeowner was about forty-one times that of the median renter[3]—even after the housing crash that supposedly proved that renting is smarter.

Of course, that's a bit of a misleading statistic in the sense that it doesn't take into account the fact that most homeowners earn more than most renters and are older than most renters. Still, when you break it down by income, the contrast is pretty amazing. The average homeowner with an income of between $16,000 and $29,999 has a net worth of $112,600. The average renter in that income range is worth only $4,240. Among people with incomes more than $80,000 per year, the average homeowner is worth $451,200; the average renter is worth just $87,400.

"But," people always say, "what if home prices stay relatively flat? Weren't the double digit annual price increases of the first part of the 2000s a one-time thing?"

They were; but owning a home will still make sense. In a Trulia survey conducted in February 2011—following the greatest housing market beat-down in U.S. history—78 percent of Americans who owned homes said that it was the best investment they'd ever made.[4] The primary benefits of homeownership have more to do with ninth-grade math than with the gyrations of the global economy.

Think about it this way: If you buy a house with 20 percent down, own it for thirty years, and your monthly expenses are roughly equivalent to what it would have cost you to rent, you will have turned your 20 percent stake in the house into a 100 percent stake in the house over thirty years.

This is the "miracle of amortization"—each month that you send in payments toward the mortgage you are paying off that mortgage and building up equity in the house. It's a form of forced savings and, over the long term, will provide you with a massive nest egg that you didn't even realize you were building as you paid the mortgage each month. Plus, you have to live somewhere, so you'll have to choose whether to rent—and pay money to your landlord so that he or she can build equity—or own, and build equity for yourself. The choice is yours.

Of course, it's not quite that simple. What if the choice is between renting for $1,000 per month or owning for . . . well, what is the cost when you add up the mortgage, taxes, insurance, water, maintenance, repairs, big repairs, major repairs, and nightmare repairs? If you figure all that will also work out to $1,000 a month, then it's a no-brainer . . . but it often costs more to own, in the short run, even allowing for the mortgage interest and property taxes that might save you some money on taxes. And there's this: You're young. You might be changing jobs a few times, getting married, moving across the country. Selling a home, even if it's easy—and the last few years it hasn't been—can easily cost 10 percent of the sales price. If you sell three or four years after you buy, this will probably leave you worse off than if you'd rented.

Still, the leverage in a low-interest, fixed-rate mortgage taken out to buy a home at a bargain price is compelling.

Say you put 20 percent down and take out a thirty-year fixed-rate mortgage. First off, because of the forced saving, the $30,000 you put down (say) will turn into $150,000 if the home value stays flat. But there's never been a thirty-year period when home prices haven't gone up by a lot, if only because of inflation. So you might find that your $30,000 investment is worth $365,000, if inflation compounds at 3 percent . . . or $650,000 if, on top of that, there's 2 percent annual appreciation reflecting increased demand and/or desirability of the neighborhood (who wouldn't want to live near you?) . . . or $65 billion if we ever have some kind of God-forbid-hyperinflation . . . or not. But with home prices low and interest rates low, it's hard to not get excited about the prospects of homeownership.

Alternatively, you could rent forever and own nothing. This is why there are really almost no rich people in America who have never owned real estate. So whenever someone talks about how renting is actually smarter, I ask him or her to show me all the people who get rich renting while never earning large incomes. *They don't exist.*

And it's getting worse. In May 2011, CNNMoney reported that "From 2006 to 2009, rental prices on average increased by more than 15 percent, according to Moody's Analytics economist Andreas Carbacho-Burgos."[5] That was in the midst of a housing meltdown, and rents are expected to continue to increase as Gen Yers opt (or are forced) to continue renting.

Homeownership with a fixed-rate mortgage provides protection against rising rents. Every month when you make a payment, some money goes to pay down the mortgage; that builds your equity in the property and, by extension, your net worth. Sure, you could just put the money in a savings account, but most people won't. The money is there but you can't spend it easily. If you put the money in the bank or even in a mutual fund, it becomes very easy to spend it. If you develop a drug addiction, you're more likely to keep your financial situation intact if you have your money in a house instead of in cash. That's right: Homeownership can prevent drug abuse or, at the very least, allow you to quit the habit sooner.

These are all of the reasons that Warren Buffett (the greatest investor in the history of the planet and among the wealthiest people in the world) has said his house was one of the top three investments of his life—the other two being wedding rings. In a 2011 letter, Buffett reflected on the home he's lived in for the past fifty-two years; he originally paid $31,500 for it, and has stayed living in it even as his net worth has grown to be 1,492,063 times the value of that house.

"For the $31,500 I paid for our house, my family and I gained fifty-two years of terrific memories with more to come," he wrote.[6]

His advice for would-be homeowners? "Instead of buying dream homes, the goal should be to buy a home you can afford." Even with all the benefits of homeownership, they simply do not outweigh the risk that comes with taking out a mortgage you can't afford. A home is a place to make memories, and whether the living room has laminate or hardwood floors has no impact on that. Your experience will be determined by the people you bring into your home, not the size of the bathroom.

Homeownership turned into an albatross for many Americans over the past few years. But without meaning to sound ghoulish about it—good for you! You missed all that (your folks may not have been so fortunate) and get to start with a clean slate. The truth is, most of the drama could have been avoided by following a few basic rules:

> **Compare total monthly costs to renting.** When long-term-oriented real estate investors evaluate property, there's one overarching thing that they're looking for: cash flow. Before they buy a property, they look at how much they can get for the property in rent each month, and then compare that to what the mortgage, taxes, and maintenance expenses and/or condo or co-op fees will be. If your monthly expenses on a house work out to $1,500 and a comparable property only rents for $800 per month, you're probably better off renting. If you live in a city like New York or San Francisco, the economics of housing prices likely mean that it will make more sense to rent; this is, incidentally, why living in a city is a really, really hard way to build wealth—and why, according to research by Dr. Thomas J. Stanley, self-made million-aires are much more likely to live outside of major high cost-of-living cities. The most inflated markets in the country also had the most out-of-whack cost of ownership versus renting ratios—and they took the biggest plunge. Comparing the cost of owning to the cost of renting is a really effective way to gauge whether the housing market you are looking at is overvalued and primed for collapse. Markets where home prices tracked closely with rentals have seen little of the carnage that has run through the real estate

market over the past few years. Incidentally, looking at real estate now in the wake of the meltdown means that this measure will tell you to buy now; at the height of the market, it would have told you not to buy. As home values fall, rental rates rise. Bloomberg reports that "for all the attention given to almost $4-a-gallon gas, the biggest threat to containing U.S. inflation may be the shift away from homeownership, which is pushing up the cost of leases across the nation's 38 million rented residences."[7] Homeownership gives you a powerful hedge against inflation.

Don't buy a house you can't afford. This one is closely related to the rule above. The idea that "A house is an investment!" enabled many Americans to rationalize buying houses they couldn't afford. For instance, eHow.com advised readers to "Buy the best house you can afford."[8] This was a sentiment echoed by many Realtors and media pundits during the boom years. Many, many people literally ruined their lives by overextending themselves on real estate. It's much better to be conservative. The general rule of thumb is that your housing costs shouldn't exceed about 28 percent of your monthly income; look at that as an outer limit though, not as a target. The lower your monthly housing costs, the greater your freedom. That freedom is more valuable than an extra bathroom.

Try to find an up-and-coming neighborhood. The best investments in real estate come when you buy a place right on the cusp of its rise to being a "higher status" neighborhood. You're young, you can rust fast, and who would mug you? What have you got to steal? Michael Corbett, author of *Before You Buy: The Homebuyer's Handbook for Today's Market*, has a clever trick for scouting out neighborhoods: "Look for places where Starbucks or Whole Foods Markets have just recently opened," he writes. "You can bet that big chains like

Starbucks spend a lot of money and time analyzing neighbor-hood potential before they open up a new store. Go ahead, tap into their market research and be their neighbor."[9]

Get a home based on what you need. Bob and Judy Haug, a couple profiled in Janet Luhrs's book *The Simple Living Guide*, gave up their big house, boats, and cars to move to a tiny apartment in their own basement. They rent the main part of the house and live in tiny quarters with exactly what they need and nothing more. Bob offered this advice to pro-spective home builders and buyers: "When you're planning a house, start with what you actually [use] instead of what your preconceived ideas are, so what you . . . use is really functional."[10] In other words, don't decide you need a family room because "That's just what people do!"

Never, ever, ever get anything other than a fixed-rate mort-gage . . . ever. If you don't know what your payments are going to be, how could you possibly know if you can afford them? If you get a fixed-rate loan and rates go down a lot, you can probably refinance. But if you get a variable-rate loan and they go up? You're screwed and maybe homeless. You will be able to afford a nicer house and have lower payments if you go with an adjustable-rate mortgage. But if rates go up, you'll find yourself living in cardboard box outside of a diner in a bad neighborhood. Don't take that risk. Please, for the love of everything, stick with a fixed-rate mortgage.

Don't fall in love with a piece of real estate. "I am as sus-ceptible to houses as some people are susceptible to other human beings," wrote early twentieth-century novelist Katharine Butler Hathaway. "Twice in my life I have fallen in love with one. Each time it was as violent and fatal as fall-ing in love with a human being." You'll get much better rest in a small bedroom surrounded by candles and beautiful prints that you bought at flea markets than you will in a custom-designed master bedroom that keeps you up at night worrying about how the hell you're going to pay for it.

A mobile home is not an investment. In certain parts of the country, mobile homes are popular. There's nothing wrong with living in one, but from an investment perspective, buying a trailer is more like buying a car than it is like buying a house. The depreciation on those things is phenomenal so if you're in the market for a mobile home, follow the advice in chapter 6 on cars: buy an older used one with cash. Incidentally, there's a guy named Lonnie Scruggs who's written some fantastic books on how to buy and maintain and possibly even make money with mobile homes. Google him if you're thinking about buying a trailer.

Recognize that, like so many things in life, your home is what you make it. It never ceases to amaze me the number of people who stretched to buy homes they couldn't really afford—and then barely took care of them or decorated them with Thomas Kinkade prints or similar atrocities. Please don't be one of these people. Look at how much it would cost you per month for your stretch house and then compare that to the monthly costs of a more affordable property. What could you do with that money? Chances are that, spent right, it could make the less desirable home a better place to live than the "better" one. Think of the stuff you could plant outside that would grow lush and beautiful, mostly on God's nickel. I spent a lot of time—and had a ton of fun—decorating the condo I own in Amherst. It's surrounded with things that are interesting and beautiful to me—and to the current tenant who asked whether the unit was available furnished——but didn't cost much. The best investment I've ever made? The candle collection that burns while I write this. Yes, you're learning about money from someone whose best investment is burning up in front of him.

Find out how much the seller paid. For the next few years, while we deal with the fallout from the rise and fall of the real estate bubble, many people will be selling their homes for little more than what they paid for them—if they're lucky. For many sellers, that amount is going to represent a psychological "peg" and will be the lowest they're willing to take for the house. It's always good to know how much a seller paid before you make your offer. The real estate agent might be able to tell you; if not, you can check Zillow.com or check with the county courthouse. Home sale prices are a matter of public record in the United States.

Better still, buy it from the bank. No emotional peg there.

Get an inspection. For somewhere between $200 and $400 or so—depending on the market and the size/complexity of the home—you can hire a home inspector to evaluate the property before you buy it—and tell you whether there's anything wrong with it, how urgent it is, and what it will cost to make repairs. Realtors will be happy to suggest a home inspector, but find your own on the Internet, or by asking someone you know. An inspector referred by an agent has an incentive to make sure the deal closes to please that agent. Consciously or subconsciously, he may not paint as bleak a picture as may be warranted. (See: *Bleak House*, by Charles Dickens, who, not having Internet access, fell into exactly this trap.)

Is a House an Investment? Kinda, Sorta, Up to a Point

One of the myths of the real estate bubble was that a house was an investment—the bigger the house you bought, the bigger the investment it was. Real estate agents all over the country urged buyers to stretch. A bigger house is a bigger investment!

It all seemed too good to be true and, of course, it was—unless you were the real estate agent collecting commissions. Which leads me to my maxim of homeownership as an investment: A home is really only an investment to the extent that, once you include the equity you're building in the house and any tax savings you might be getting, it ends up costing you the same amount each month as renting.

The best real estate investment is most likely a relatively small, affordable, entry-level house or condominium in an older neighborhood. When buying a condominium, make sure that the complex has a stable financial situation with adequate reserves and fewer than 5 percent of the units having gone into foreclosure during the past three years. If you're going to buy a condo—which I think is really the best thing for young people with active lifestyles—there are two books worth checking out: Gary W. Eldred's *Make Money with Condominiums and Townhouses* and Andris Virsnieks's *How to Invest in Condominiums: The Low-Risk Option for Long-Term Cash Flow.*

How Much House to Buy?

When it comes to buying a house, the old-school rules are the way to go. How old school, you ask? In 1953, *New York Post* personal finance columnist Sylvia Porter cowrote a book called *Managing Your Money* that was, for many years, the most widely read money book on the planet. When it comes to deciding how much home you can afford she advises you to "take annual income and multiply by two—or two and a half, at most. Is income $4,500 a year? Then to be safe, a house should not cost more than $9,000 to $11,200."[11]

Now I know what you're thinking: These numbers are dated and irrelevant. "I'm a recent grad and this is the year 2012! I'll be in my fifties by the time I'm earning $4,500 per year!"

If you live in New York City or San Francisco, these numbers probably won't work. But in most parts of the country, you will likely be able to find an affordable entry-level house or condominium at a price that falls within these 1953 guidelines. They're old-fashioned but they would have helped people avoid a lot of the tragic problems they got into a few years ago. So, if you are single and have an income of $40,000 per year, you should be looking for a home that costs no more than $80,000–$100,000. Married with a combined income of $100,000? Then, $200,000–$250,000 should be your range. These numbers seem conservative and they are, but they sure beat ending up homeless with trashed credit.

Some of the happiest people I know—and yes, I really do know people like this—are those who keep their housing expenses way, way below that guideline: people who earn $500,000 per year but live in $120,000 homes. As Picasso said, "I'd like to live as a poor man with lots of money." The lower your fixed expenses, the freer you feel.

In Amherst, Massachusetts, the median home price is $331,000—substantially higher than the median home price nationwide. But the two-bedroom condo I own cost just $125,000, and there are fewer drug deals in my neighborhood than you might think.

Bring Your Parents to Look at Houses?

It can be tempting to rely on your parents for help with picking a house. But just because they're your parents doesn't mean that they actually know *anything*. Plus, there are all kinds of dynamics at work when you add your parents to the process. Your dad is probably an idiot, but he'll want to sound smart by talking about "cracks in the foundation" or "insect damage" or "dated appliances" or any other buzzwords he heard while watching HGTV in his underwear. Unless your parents really know a ton about real estate, or you really want them to come, I think it's best to leave them at home.

One home inspector who asked not to be identified told me that parents love to mess things up when they come along for an inspection. "I'll be trying to work and they'll be pointing to a scratch in the wall while I'm trying to look at an electrical problem that could kill someone," he told me. "They don't know anything and they're distracting."

And when it comes to picking an assisted living facility for the old folks, you definitely don't want them to come. You'll want to pick based on price, but they can easily interfere by asking meddlesome questions about things like health codes, indoor plumbing, and corporal punishment.

Use a Real Estate Agent

Whether real estate agents are worth using when you're selling is an open question; I don't cover selling a house in this book because chances are you're nowhere close to the age where you'll sell your first house. But as a buyer, the choice is clear: Use a real estate agent. You don't pay the agent; the seller does. Typically, that commission is 5 or 6 percent, split between the seller's agent and your own.

To find a real estate agent, asks friends in your area, or log on to NAEBA.org to find someone who specializes in representing buyers. I recommend going with the one with the best hair. But some people prefer to look for someone with experience. Here are some things to think about:

> **How long has the real estate agent lived in the area?** The biggest benefit from Realtors, I've found, is their knowledge of the area: what's close to what, whether the Chinese restaurant near the house you're buying is any good, and what the reputations of various neighborhoods are. If you're relatively new to an area, this knowledge is invaluable. Try to avoid agents who are new to town.
>
> **What are his or her credentials?** You want a real estate agent who stays on the cutting edge of the industry. Look for one who has credentials like Graduate Realtors Institute (GRI), Certified Residential Specialist (CRS), and Accredited Buyer Representative (ABR). These aren't guarantees of excellence, but they're better than a poke in the eye.

Get references. You really don't want to hire a Realtor until you've read endorsements from—or better yet, spoken with—people who've worked with him or her in the past. This is why the best way to find a real estate agent is to ask friends who have bought or sold a home.

Background check! Check with your state's real estate licensing board to find out whether your prospective real estate agent has complaints that have resulted in disciplinary action. Not all states have this information searchable online, but try googling your state's real estate board to find out.

Avoid dual agency. Dual agency is the technical term for the situation when a real estate agent represents both the buyer and the seller. For instance, if you go to an open house on your own and decide to make an offer with that real estate agent representing you, you have entered into a dual agency situation. In some states this is legal and in some states it isn't; it's always a bad idea for the buyer, though. You want your real estate agent to represent you exclusively—and, no, there is no money to be saved by using the seller's agent. Ann Brenoff, the *Huffington Post*'s real estate writer, puts it this way: "A seller wants every last nickel he can squeeze from the sale of his house and a buyer wants to avoid overpaying by that very same nickel. How can one person really represent both those interests at the same time?"[12] Always, always have your own real estate agent represent you.

Consider using an exclusive buyer's agent. One way to avoid this conflict entirely is to work with a real estate agent who doesn't take listings him- or herself. The National Association of Exclusive Buyer Agents has a directory of agents who are devoted exclusively to working with buyers. Check out NAEBA.org to learn more.

Avoid for Sale by Owner Homes

Many people think that buying something for sale by owner (FSBO) is a great way to find a bargain. Knock on doors, respond to "For Sale" signs, and find a bargain! And save on the real estate commission. What could go wrong? A lot.

This is generally not a good idea, especially for, to borrow a phrase from one of my favorite HGTV shows, a *property virgin*. You're not going to get a good deal in most cases because the reason people opt to sell their homes on their own is that they want to get as much money out of the sale as they possibly can.

I once bought a condo from a woman who was selling it herself without an agent and, bless her heart, this lady was insane. She had knitted "cozies" to cover the air conditioner in the bedroom and was offering to include them as part of her counteroffer. Scary, scary, *American Psycho*–type stuff, but they were lovely cozies and I still have them. This is pretty typical of what you'll encounter if you try to buy a home through a FSBO.

As a first-time home buyer, you really, really want the benefit of a real estate agent who knows what he or she is doing. They are worth the money, not least because it's the seller who pays it.

Federal Housing Administration Loans

OK, so you ran the numbers on your area and have determined that owning your own house or condo is likely to be comparable in cost to renting. You're planning to stay in the same area for at least five years.

Obviously, you can't afford to pay cash for an entire house so you're going to need to get a mortgage. The best thing is to put down at least 20 percent. However, on a $150,000 starter home or condo, that's $30,000, plus closing costs. For many young people, it will take a prohibitively long period of time to come up with that much cash.

There is an alternative: a Federal Housing Administration

(FHA) loan (or a Veteran's Administration [VA] loan, if you happen to be a veteran). You can buy a home or condo with a down payment of as little as 3.5 percent, and a credit score as low as 580—approximately 90 percent of Americans have credit scores that good, so it's not a big hurdle. And the interest rates on FHA loans are generally comparable to what you'd get with a conventional loan.

In her book *The New Rules for Mortgages*, Dale Robyn Siegel advises those seeking an FHA loan to go with "an experienced lender and never want to pay more than 1 percent in points, origination, or discount fees." A few more things to consider:

> **Don't just put down 3.5 percent.** If you can come up with 20 percent, you can avoid paying extra each month for private mortgage insurance. The more you put down, the lower your monthly payments will be and the less interest you'll pay.
>
> **Recognize the fees included.** When you take out an FHA loan, you will have to pay a fee of 1 percent of the total loan amount for insurance; then, every year, you will have to pay more each month for insurance until you have built up equity of 22 percent of the home's value. This isn't necessarily a huge deal, but you do need to keep it in mind and find out from your banker exactly how much the insurance will cost before you get too far into the process of buying. Also, note that this insurance protects the lender, not you, in the event that you default on the mortgage.
>
> **Go with a credit union.** Find a local credit union (use CUlookup.com or ask around) to handle your mortgage. Why? Because they are, frankly, more competent than the big national banks. To wit: In March 2010, Bank of America accidentally broke into a house they thought was in foreclosure (it wasn't), cut off the utilities, padlocked the door, and kidnapped the homeowner's parrot.[13] Sure, that kind of thing

could happen with any bank, but it only seems to happen with the big national banks, which are run by morons.

Ask yourself if you're really ready. FHA loans can be a great way for someone who is young, doesn't have a big down payment, and hasn't yet built up a really high credit score to get an entry-level home with an affordable down payment. But please: Don't buy a home with an FHA loan until you are car-loan, credit card debt, and, ideally, student loan free. There are all kinds of ads about buying a home with bad credit; it's a lot harder to do than it used to be, which is good. One of the silver linings of the real estate crisis is that the people who really shouldn't buy homes aren't able to the way they used to be.

Rent Versus Buy Calculator

There are tons of online calculators to help you decide whether to rent or buy. The best of them is this one from the *New York Times*: http://www.nytimes.com/interactive/business/buy-rent-calculator .html.

The basic framework is this: Compare your current monthly rent to the cost of the mortgage, property taxes, insurance, and any homeowner's association fees for the property you're thinking about buying. Also, add a little bit for maintenance costs. If renting is much cheaper than owning—and in markets like New York City it is—then keep renting. But if your credit is in good shape, you're planning to stay in the area for at least the next five years, and you have enough in savings for a down payment, you really need to think about buying.

While You're Renting

For most recent grads, homeownership is at least a few years away. There's nothing wrong with that, and it would be a terrible mistake to rush into homeownership before you have the stability and savings to do it. And, in fact, if you live in a high-priced city, it may make more sense for you to rent for the foreseeable future. This is not the time to be looking for the home with the best features. Find something safe, reasonably clean, and in a reasonably convenient location. Then, put a few bucks into paint (with the landlord's permission or, even better, get him or her to pay for the paint if you'll do the labor), flowers, and candles, and call it home—for now.

Here are a few ideas for getting the best deals on rentals, along with some important things to remember:

Scour Craigslist for properties owned by mom-and-pop landlords. Often, these are the best deals and they're especially good if you don't have the best credit history. If the landlord just likes you—and how could he *not?*—that will help, too.

Negotiate! This varies considerably from market to market, and rental housing is currently much, much stronger than the sales market. Just because the housing market in your area is depressed doesn't mean the rental market is. But it's still worth trying to get a better deal. The best way to do this is to come prepared with information to show the landlord that his or her property is priced high compared to similar properties.

Offer to work in exchange for reduced rent. Painting, landscaping, trash duties—ask the landlord or property manager and see whether there's any work you can do around the property in exchange for reduced rent. Don't like the walls in your unit? Many landlords—including me!—will offer to pay for all of the supplies if a tenant wants to paint a room, as long as he picks a tasteful color.

Be a home health aid. If you happen to have some basic health care training, you may be able to get a job living with/

assisting an elderly person part-time and live rent free. These jobs aren't real easy to find, but they are out there.

Never pay for more than the first month, the last month, and a security deposit equal to about one month's rent up front. So if you're renting an $800 per month apartment, you shouldn't have to put down more than about $2,400 when you sign the lease. Some landlords—especially mom-and-pop types who are renting out their own home or a one-off investment property—will want you to prepay more up front or will offer you a big discount if you pay, for instance, six months of rent in advance. Never do this; it is a sign that the landlord is in financial distress and, if the property goes into foreclosure, you will be evicted and end up homeless and have no way of getting back all that money you paid in rent.

If you have a very limited credit history, some landlords may make it difficult to sign a lease. This is most likely to be a problem with large apartment complexes; small, mom-and-pop landlords are likely to give you some leeway. Another possible solution is to submit your application with a few letters of recommendation from a former landlord, a minister, or an employer or professor who can attest to your reliability and character. There are also companies like Insurent.com that, in exchange for a fee, will effectively cosign your application and agree to pay up if you default on the lease. You probably shouldn't use this service because you probably don't need to, but it's an option to be aware of.

Read the lease thoroughly before signing. Ah. Just when the landlord was beginning to like you. But don't sign the lease on the spot; take it home and read it. If you have a friend or relative who's involved in real estate, ask him or her to look it over. It's generally a good idea to try to get the landlord to insert a clause giving you the right to terminate the lease early in exchange for a penalty—one or two months' rent—in the event that you need to move for a job change. If you're in an area with high demand and low vacancy, this isn't as important: the landlord will be able to find a replacement tenant quickly. But if you're renting an apartment in Chernobyl or Biloxi and you don't have this clause, you could theoretically get stuck paying rent for an extra year while you're across the country.

If your maintenance requests aren't being responded to, document them. The tough economy encourages many landlords to be extra stingy. If you make a request to have something repaired because the issue makes the home unlivable—a non-working refrigerator, broken heater in Fargo in the middle of December, toilet clogged on taco night—you may have the right to have the repair taken care of yourself, and then deduct the cost from your next rent payment by attaching a copy of the receipt along with a note of explanation. This is a drastic and adversarial way of handling it, but sometimes it's your only option. However, never, ever decline to pay the rent because you're having an issue with your landlord. This will get you evicted and trash your credit.

Always be there with the landlord for the walk-through when you move in and for the walk-through when you move out. This is where the landlord will assess the condition of the unit and charge you for damages. If you aren't there to dispute anything in person, it can be very, very difficult to contest any issues. In the current market—where many people have lost a lot of money on their real estate investments—a lot of unscrupulous landlords are basically trying to steal people's security deposits by making up bogus repairs. So before you move out, clean very thoroughly, and take pictures—with a time stamp on them—to show the condition of the unit. If the landlord doesn't return your deposit within thirty days, send a letter demanding it back; after that, your only option is small claims court.

Roommates

If you're renting, having roommates is almost always the way to go—you keep costs down, split utilities, have company, and you're able to save a larger chunk of your income toward a down payment on your own place.

But, when you decide to share a living space and the financial responsibilities that come with doing that, it can really go one of two ways: *Golden Girls* or *Jerry Springer*.

There are four words you need to know about this: *joint and several liability*.

Those are the four most dangerous words in the English language—narrowly beating out "cosigned on car loan" and "Is that an M-16?" What these four words mean is that when you sign a lease with your roommates, you are each fully responsible for the entire amount—and if you signed a lease with an idiot, his or her low IQ points will essentially be deducted from your bank account and then multiplied by the length of your lease and subtracted from your credit score.

So if you and your friends Jenna, Ehud, and Pedro lease a house together for $3,000 per month, and then Jenna, Ehud, and Pedro skip town and stop contributing toward the rent, you are still responsible for the entire $3,000 per month. That's what joint and several liability means. You are all collectively responsible for the rent (jointly) and each of you is also, as an individual, legally responsible for the entire amount of the rent (severally).

If you end up sharing a lease with the wrong people—say, Lenny Dykstra, Teresa Giudice, and MC Hammer—you could be in for a life-altering financial disaster. Here's how to ensure that that doesn't happen, and how to make living with roommates something other than a disaster:

Pull credit reports together before you fill out a lease application. The landlord will almost certainly run a credit check on everyone on the lease, but if you have great credit and your roommate has horrible credit, the landlord may let you rent an apartment without your ever knowing that your "business partner" in this deal is a disaster. When deciding who you're going to live with, sit down and check each other's credit scores together on a site like MyFico.com. It costs less than $20. You don't need someone with a credit score of 800; you just want to make sure that you're not getting involved with someone who has a track record of skipping out on bills.

Always pay your share of the rent directly to the landlord. One of my friends lives in New York City and shares an apartment with a friend he's known since college. Sadly, his friend became a major drug addict during the time they lived together—my friend would pay this guy his share of the rent each month ($1,000) and this guy was supposed to then pay the landlord. You probably see where this is going, but the roommate used my friend's money to buy drugs and then hid the eviction notices that eventually arrived after he stopped paying rent. And because the lease is a joint and several agreement, the fact that my friend paid the money to his roommate doesn't help him with the landlord—who will probably sue him for thousands of dollars in rent, plus court costs and interest. Theoretically, my friend could then sue his roommate for misappropriating the money he paid him for rent. But given that his roommate's assets consist of empty pill bottles, an Easy-Bake Oven, and three seasons of

Will & Grace on VHS, that's probably not a strategy worth pursuing. The key point to remember is this: The fact that his roommate ripped him off doesn't change my friend's liability to the landlord. Bottom line: *Never* pay money for rent to anyone other than the person you owe that money to as part of your lease agreement. Really. Just don't do it. It's sloppy, and it works fine until it stops working, and then when it stops working look out because it *really* stops working.

Speak up at the first sign of trouble. If your roommate is not keeping current with the rent, talk to him or her *and* talk to the landlord to assess your options. It's just too important to worry about being diplomatic. Paying rent late regularly can hurt your credit, cost you a lot of money in fees, and make it impossible for you to secure a lease for your next apartment.

CHAPTER 8

Joint Venture Partners: Money and Sex

Shortly before the publication of my first book, I found myself dating someone who was, to put it mildly, a financial disaster. He earned a very good income but had credit collectors calling his phone and, on our second date, he went to pay for something only to find that Chase had emptied his checking account via court order. Hot.

"Well, this is kinda cool," my mother said when I told her about him. "You're a financial expert. This is what you do. You help people solve these problems. And now you can help him!"

Well, not exactly, I reminded her. Can you imagine if some psychopathic ax murderer asked her out on a date and I said, "Go for it! He's *nuts*! You're *professionally trained in helping people who are nuts*! This is a match made in heaven!"

But my own relationship money drama was nothing compared to the reigning king and queen (divorced—which just proves my point) of the world of relationship drama. There was so much wrong between Jon and Kate Gosselin that finances wasn't the first problem people thought about when their marriage unraveled. In the wake of their divorce though, money took a starring role. A lot of money. According to Jon, between 2005 and 2009 the couple accrued more than $2 million. Also, according to Jon, "Kate handled all the banking."

"She's hiding money," he said in response to allegations that he had left her broke by withdrawing money from their joint account. "We have eleven bank accounts. That was just our joint account."[1]

Eighty-four percent of couples say that money is a source of tension in the home; in a large percentage of those cases, that tension leads to arguments, divorce, and cameos on *Cops* lying face down in a pool of pepper spray in a bad neighborhood. Different ideas about handling money, and the distrust that often comes because of it, can tear a relationship apart. But if you can get on the same page about money, the rewards can be fantastic.

Dr. Thomas J. Stanley has surveyed thousands of millionaires over the years. He's consistently found that a stable relationship is one of the most important factors that contributes to the ability to build wealth. In *The Millionaire Mind*, he writes that "92 percent of the millionaire households in America are composed of a married couple and these millionaire couples have less than one-third the divorce rate of nonmillionaire couples."

A few years ago, Mara, thirty-nine, and Frankie, thirty-six, Sachs found themselves $30,000 in debt, and Mara felt like she was the only one who cared.

"I was definitely more psychologically affected by it than my husband because I was the one getting the mail and handling the bills," she told me. "We were staying on top of it on paper and it looked like we had it under control but in my head and in my sweat glands it was bad."

With the help of Dave Ramsey's book *The Total Money Makeover*, Mara and Frankie got themselves out of debt—and strengthened their relationship in the process. She even started a blog, KosherOnABudget.com, where she chronicles the family's efforts to achieve a solid financial life.

"We realized we were spending $1,000 a month more than we were taking in. So we cut our expenses down to nothing," she says. "The hardest thing for my husband was getting rid of cable."

In the long run, the reduced stress and feelings of being on the same page about budgeting brought the couple closer together. "I don't hate my mailbox anymore," Mara said, referring to the days when they didn't have enough money to pay the electric bill.

Surveys consistently show that money issues are among the leading causes of divorce. So how can you use money to bring each other closer together instead of farther apart?

Both of you need to be in it together. As Jon Gosselin learned, leaving your partner in charge of the finances can lead to disaster. "Often, one member of the couple is aware of the detailed finances, while the other lives in fantasy land and becomes angry at his/her penny-pinching mate," says family and divorce lawyer Laurie Puhn, author of *Fight Less, Love More: 5-Minute Conversations to Change Your Relationship Without Blowing Up or Giving In.* "It becomes a parent–child relationship because the responsible mate is setting limits on the irresponsible mate. Instead, both people must take responsibility for understanding the finances." It's fine if one person is more into making the spreadsheets, but you both need to be equal partners in the decision-making and planning process. To underscore this, Dave Ramsey's Financial Peace University program generally does not allow married people to enroll without bringing their spouse along, too. Money is a team sport.

Recognize that there are significant challenges to being in a relationship with someone who is your financial opposite. In a study called "Fatal (Fiscal) Attraction," Scott Rick, of the Ross School of Business at the University of Michigan, Deborah Small of the Wharton School of the University of Pennsylvania, and Eli Finkel of Northwestern University surveyed couples about their financial habits and their relationships. They found that most people *claim* that their ideal partner is someone with similar financial habits, but people are actually statistically more likely to marry someone who is their complete financial opposite. And people in a relationship with their financial opposite are less likely to be satisfied with their relationships.[2]

Never let your smarter, more financially sophisticated partner handle everything. It can be tempting—like if you're, say, a kindergarten teacher and your wife is a financial planner—but you really need to make sure that you're aware of what's going on in your financial life. *New York Times* business columnist Eilene Zimmerman made this mistake, in spite of her own career writing about money, and wrote about it in a piece for Salon.com. When her twenty-year marriage ended in divorce, her lack of knowledge of her and her spouse's financial situation created a mess.[3]

Focus on reality, not on opinions. It's easy to get into the blame game when you're talking about money issues. But that can put the other person on the defensive and cause him or her to shut down. "The key is to focus on the facts, rather than the emotions," Puhn said in *Fighting Less, Love More*. Instead of telling your boyfriend or girlfriend that it's ridiculous for him or her to be wasting $300 per year on *NFL Sunday Ticket*, show him or her how much money you're spending versus how much you're making, and ask him or her to come up with ideas for cuts. That might sound petty, but the point is that you need to bring him or her to the table, not offer up ultimatums or orders.

Don't lie. It's sad that this has to be said but it does. A 2011 survey conducted by CESI Debt Solutions shows an alarmingly high level of financial infidelity among married couples (a possible explanation for the high divorce rate). Eighteen and a half percent of married people have a secret credit card that their spouse doesn't know about. Clothing is the number one secret purchase, with 19.9 percent of secret spenders concerned that their marriage might end if their partner became aware of the purchases. Follow Warren Buffett's rule about integrity: If you're not sure whether your partner would be OK with you doing something, ask him or her. If you have to ask, you probably already know the answer. Also, if your partner is hiding financial stuff, that's a huge red flag about his or her character. *Integrity is rarely compartmentalized.*

In the beginning, try to make it fun. If you're fairly early in a relationship, your finances aren't comingled enough that you need to be budgeting together. Still, find an opportunity to tackle a financial challenge together. "Too many couples spend thirty years nagging each other about money. Who wants to live like that? Instead, for your first money decision, pick something FUN to work towards," says Ramit Sethi of IWillTeachYouToBeRich.com. "Maybe it's a trip to Thailand, or a weekend getaway. In other words, don't start off negative—first, focus on the positive. Then you can start doing the important work of paying off debt together and saving for long-term goals."

This is all important information for couples in any relationship. What about the increasingly common problem—where someone you think you may really like has serious financial problems? According to one survey, 87 percent of men and 80 percent of women said that a bankruptcy or significant credit card debt would not impact their decision to stay in a relationship with someone.

This is heartwarming—but not smart. My tough-love advice: Don't get involved with a financial disaster. It's likely to affect your quality of life and, often, points to broader personality issues.

And if your guy or girl's financial problems are serious enough, the mind-set that got him or her into money woes will likely bleed over into other aspects of his or her life. For instance, that guy or girl who leases a flashy car he or she can barely afford? There's a good chance he or she is a narcissist, according to Dr. Jean Twenge, co-author of *The Narcissism Epidemic*.

"Going into debt allows people to look better off than they actually are, so narcissists love credit," she says. "Overspending is very typical of narcissistic people. They favor image over saving and fantasy over reality,"

"Put simply, a narcissist will break your heart," she adds. "Relationships with narcissists tend to start out fine and then you slowly come to realize that this person has himself at the center of his universe and doesn't truly care for others. Instead of having at the center of their relationship being caring about each other, they enjoy playing games back and forth."

A study out of the University of Texas at San Antonio found that men who drove flashy cars or otherwise consumed conspicuously tended to be interested only in short-term sexual relationships.[4]

And, if you're among those tempted to spend lavishly to try to attract the opposite sex, be careful: It doesn't work as well as people think. Professor Daniel Beal, a coauthor of the study, put it this way in a press release: "When women considered him for a long-term relationship, owning the sports car held no advantage relative to owning an economy car. . . . People may feel that owning flashy things makes them more attractive as a relationship partner, but in truth, many men might be sending women the wrong message."

And guys, don't think you're fooling anyone. Women who participated in the study had the same reaction to men who lived lavishly: they weren't considered that interesting.[5] The real chick magnet is a car without a loan.

Because millionaires are abnormally successful financially and in terms of their ability to build relationships that last, they can be a good source of tips on choosing a partner. Dr. Stanley asked millionaires to list the attributes that contributed to their successful marriages. The top five responses—among both men and women—were that their spouses were honest, responsible, loving, capable, and supportive. Honesty and responsibility also ranked high on millionaires' list of traits that enabled them to achieve success. Find someone who's good with money and you've probably found someone who's good relationship material in lots of other ways, too.

If you're in a relationship with a financial messs, I'm sorry. Next time, be sure to listen to first lady of finance Suze Orman who warns, "FICO before sex." Find out if the guy or girl is a financial fit—or at least not a human Enron—before you roll around in the hay.

Remember, if you want a fixer-upper, look for it in a house, not a spouse. My grandfather once told my mother that "It's just as easy to fall in love with a rich man as a poor one!" That's a little cynical. And actually sort of creepy. I think I see his point, though. The idea is not to find a rich partner, but you need to avoid people with dangerous financial habits. People build powerful financial platforms from all income levels, but someone who doesn't understand the real benefits of wealth is not a good match for you. I think you deserve better, solely because you bought this book.

Here are some additional important tips:

Keep your money separate until you're married. File this one under trust in God but lock your doors. Until you're married and are joined as one legally, it's much, much safer to keep your money separate. If you're sharing rent on an apartment, you should each cut a separate check to the landlord (if he or she balks, blame me). There is just no reason to be comingling funds with someone you're not married to. It's tempting, but there are just so many ways it can go wrong. Also, I hope this goes without saying, but please, please, please do not even dream of buying a home with someone you aren't married to yet. Don't do it, don't do it, don't do it, don't do it. OK? Or, have a very clear legal agreement that specifies exactly what happens when you decide you hate each other. But really. Just don't do it.

If you do get married, don't assume your spouse's debt. One writer complained that he "left college owing nothing. A few months and a wedding later, I owed $12,000. That was the price of marrying the girl of my dreams."[6] And a very small price to pay, I say. But if you do want to help, just make payments toward the loan. There is no reason for you to assume the full amount of the debt in your own name. So don't.

CHAPTER 9

Careers in Art History
(and Other One-Liners)

If you're doing something you love, an hour feels like five
minutes. If you're doing something that doesn't resonate
with your spirit, five minutes feels like an hour.

—KEN ROBINSON

Up until now, we've been talking about how to manage the money
you have—and spending. How to avoid spending too much of it,
what to do with the money you don't spend, and how to get the most
out of the money you do spend.

But, especially for recent grads, the earning part of the financial
equation is huge. If you don't have a job or a sugar daddy, no amount
of frugality is going to make this work. My editor nixed the idea of a
chapter on how to find a sugar daddy, so instead I'll talk about
careers. Wicked lame, I know, but stay with me.

If you're reading this soon after publication, the job market is
pretty bleak, I know. And it's been that way for a long time. During
the first four months of 2009, less than half of college graduates under
twenty-five were working at jobs that required a degree, according to
data from the Center for Labor Market Studies at Northeastern University in Boston.[1] The admissions office at Northeastern, one of the

most expensive schools in America, has not been incorporating this data into their marketing materials to potential students.

You might think that a book on the importance of doing well with your money would focus on earning as much money as possible. But when I look at all the data on picking a career, I conclude that choosing a career path based largely on the desire to earn a high income probably won't lead to a fulfilling outcome—certainly not personally and, interestingly, probably not financially, either. One study found that depression affects a larger percentage of the population in affluent countries than in less affluent ones.[2]

If you hate your job, you're not going to like your life. Think about it: A week consists of 168 hours. If you sleep seven hours per day, that brings you down to 119. So the average forty-hour work week takes up a third of your waking hours—and that doesn't even include the average of fifteen hours that I spend each week trying to update my Facebook privacy settings and the other five hours I devote to figuring out at what point during the day I will be able to charge my cell phone.

A three-year study conducted at the University of Aberdeen Business School in Scotland found that job satisfaction is the most important factor in determining overall satisfaction with life. It's more important than satisfaction with family, leisure time, health, finance, and social life.[3]

So by all means, take a high-paying job that you don't find fulfilling; you can join the nonexistent cohort of people who love their lives and hate their work. And lest you say, "Well I'm passionate about X and there's no possible way to make money in anything related to X," make sure you don't say it to Takeru Kobayashi. Born in Nagano, Japan, Kobayashi has a rare talent for being able to eat enormous quantities of food in very short periods of time. He also knows that Americans will watch almost anything we put on television (except for shows that were actually good like *Arrested Development*) and so, consequently, he's been able to earn a six-figure income by eating fifty hot dogs with buns in twelve minutes. He's also eaten 17.7 pounds of cow brains in fifteen minutes, and twenty pounds of rice balls in thirty minutes. "People think that if you have a huge appetite, then you'll be better at it. But actually, it's how you confront the food that is brought to you. You have to be mentally and psychologically pre-pared." His specific secret to career success? Take the hot dog out of the bun and eat it and dip the bun in 7UP so that it gets squishy and you can shove a few of them in your mouth at once. He calls it the "Solomon method," and it's something I expect will be taught in gym classes across the country within my lifetime.

If someone can get rich stuffing their face on television, then really nothing should be off the table in terms of career goals.

And Kobayashi is not the only person who has been able to get rich off of his passions. In his landmark study of America's self-made millionaires, Dr. Thomas J. Stanley found that "81 percent of [the millionaires surveyed] selected a vocation because 'My job/career allows me full use of my abilities and aptitudes.'" Dr. Stanley also found that the more wealth people had, the more likely they were to agree with the statement "My success is a direct result of loving my career or business."

Now I know what you're thinking: "But my passion is sitting at home in my underwear alternating between Paula Deen and the Outdoor Living Record while trying to beat my high score in *Angry Birds*. How can I turn that into a career?"

Figuring Out What You're Meant to Do and Doing It

One of the hardest parts of picking a career—and I know because I've experienced this issue myself—is that it can seem so abstract when you're thinking about it that it can be easy to get caught up in fantasies of who you'd like to be versus the realities of what you'd like to do. Because a career is mostly acts of doing rather than states of being, it's important to keep the superego out of this conversation.

Jon Acuff, a brilliant career expert and author of the equally brilliant book *Quitter: Closing the Gap Between Your Day Job & Your Dream Job*, told me that "a lot of times when you come to the blank slate, what do I wanna do, what do I wanna be, it's not real. The ego's really loud in that moment."

So how do you escape it?

You have to ask yourself: "What's been true of my life that I loved that I can continue to execute on that matters to me," Acuff says. In this tough job market, it's extremely important to differentiate between *passions* and *positions*.

"A position is a place in a cubicle," Acuff says. "When you chase a position, it's a really narrow path. For me, insight and ideas were what I loved to do, and that's my core passion. I could execute that in a million different ways. So I try to encourage people to not go 'I have to find this perfect job that's this position.' I'd rather say, 'Here's what I love to do, here's my core.' So how can I *do* that and then narrow it down from that very broad base?"

And when you get too fixated on a position that is unattainable at this particular moment, you can often miss out on the chance to execute on your underlying passions that may be present in your day job.

Reflecting on his past career as a cubicle-dwelling information technology worker at various companies, Acuff experienced this phenomenon himself. "A lot of times there's at least an element of that dream in that day job, but you can miss out on it because you're being negative. I'd say I want to reach people and communicate with them. And then I'd go sit in an office with people all day and ignore them."

If you're not really sure what interests you—or you're not working in a field that you find fulfilling—here are some ideas to help you move forward:

Take a trip in the way-back machine. Acuff recommends looking back to the things that interested you when you were younger—maybe things you've completely forgotten about and haven't done in years. Did you collect something? What did you do with your free time before you got caught up in the world of deadlines and quizzes and social expectations? Did you used to love cooking or fixing things, before you got too busy with drinking?

Start subscribing to magazines, e-mail lists, and blogs for careers and industries that interest you. This is great for three reasons. First, you may find out that a field you're initially drawn to becomes even more (or less, which is good information to have, too) interesting as you learn more about it and current industry trends. You also may find leads for jobs, especially in the form of interesting people. Simply getting in touch with people who are interesting and connected within an industry you're passionate about is often a much better way of landing a job than filling out endless applications. It's more circuitous, but often more effective. TradePub.com has an extensive listing of these magazines, and most of them also have websites where you can check out the articles for free.

Order some personal business cards. If you're unemployed, or underemployed, it's a good idea to have them. These should list all of your contact information, along with your major and any special skills you might have. You can get five hundred cards for less than $10 including shipping from sites like VistaPrint.com.

Keep a résumé handy whenever possible. This is easier for women and guys with man-purses than it is for the rest of us, but you never know when you'll run into someone who has a job opening that's a good fit for you or knows someone who does. I'm not saying you need to hand them out like those tools who hand out business cards at parties, but it's just a useful thing to have handy. If you need help with your résumé, there are tons of books that can help. You can also e-mail me a draft—Zbissonnette@gmail.com—and I'll let you know what I think. And keep a copy on your cell phone—you don't need a man-purse for that—so you can just shoot it over electronically.

Don't quit your day job. Unless you are debt-free and have six months' worth of living expenses, or will be able to start generating income from your dream job immediately, it's just too risky otherwise to be unemployed. It also makes you a less desirable candidate. A sensible middle-ground: try to start your dream career as a nights and weekends freelance thing. Go back and reread the section about when my dad quit his teaching job to learn about the importance of not quitting a job when you don't have any money.

Spend Less Time Filling Out Applications

I see so many young people spending countless hours hunched over their computers, guzzling Red Bull, scratching their crotches, and filling out endless numbers of online job applications.

There's nothing wrong with this approach as part of your job hunt—and, indeed, many people do manage to find jobs on Career-Builder, Monster, Craigslist, and RentBoys.com (don't look up that last one).

But I do worry that many people substitute this component of a job and career search for the other elements of it that are more important. Filling out online job applications feels productive because every time you hit "send," you might just be submitting the thing that will instantly end your job search woes.

According to the Harvard Business School's alumni affairs office, "Networking is a way to develop relationships that help you gain insight into an industry, a company, or a career path. Given that 65 to 85 percent of jobs are found through networking, it should be the focus of about 80 percent of your allotted search time."[4]

This is confusing because if 65 to 85 percent of jobs are found through networking, why would 80 percent be the percentage of your time you should devote to networking? Shouldn't it be 75 percent, as that's halfway between 65 and 85? I guess the math doesn't have to make sense when you're Harvard Business School. Anyway . . .

We already talked about reading newsletters and magazines related to the industry you're in, but as with so many things, personal connections are important. I made the connection to an agent for my first book because I e-mailed my favorite author when I was in high school and we became friends. I became a contributing editor with *Antique Trader* because I e-mailed a pitch for a freelance story to an editor there.

But here's my favorite story of how this can work out: Robert (Bobby) Lopez won a Tony award for cowriting the music and lyrics for the Broadway hit *Avenue Q.* His foot in the door to the world of musical theater came in high school, when he wrote a letter to Stephen Sondheim, one of the most legendary musical theater personalities of our time. To his astonishment, Sondheim wrote back.

"What I learned is that people do answer unsolicited letters," Lopez later told Lindsey Pollak for her wonderful book *Getting from College to Career: 90 Things to Do Before You Join the Real World.* "Everyone you respect and admire got where they got with help from people they admire. Everyone is willing to 'pay it forward.' People understand how much a word from them means."

Making connections with people in your field is one of the most important keys to having success in that field.

Here's what I want you to do: Make a list of five people you aspire to be like in your career; the more obscure, the better, because there's a better chance they'll write back. If you write to Bill Gates, you'll probably never hear anything. But if your goal is to become a leader in the restaurant industry, writing to the CEO of a small regional chain will very likely lead to a response and a phone call or meeting—and a chance to learn and, if you make a great impression, possibly even a job somewhere down the road. Your efforts to connect with people have to come from a place of sincere interest, and should be bolstered by extensive reading of trade magazines in the field.

Let's say you're interested in pursuing a career in the restaurant industry, so naturally you've been online reading *Nation's Restaurant News*, *QSR*, and *Restaurant*.

As you're browsing the *Nation's Restaurant News* website, you stumble on a very interesting article that quotes Kevin Harron, the CEO of Burtons Grill restaurant group, in an article about the upscale chain's new focus on suburban baby boomers. You keep reading to learn that Mr. Harron used to work for Outback Steakhouse and Carrabba's Italian Grill, among other chains.[5]

So here's an example of a letter you might write to Mr. Harron:

Dear Mr. Harron,

I read with great interest the story about your company's success in Nation's Restaurant News. *As a recent graduate of the University of [Wherever] with a degree in management and a long-time interest in the restaurant industry, I am impressed by restaurateurs who have succeeded in spite of these difficult times. Your restaurant's focus on locally grown foods strikes me as an innovative way for a chain to connect with a community and offer fresh options with a marketing hook that has broad appeal.*

I am in the early stages of my restaurant career; I have six years of experience working as a server at Chili's, but my long-term goal is to work at the management level at a restaurant chain. I'm sure you are extremely busy, but I would love to set up a time to talk by phone and sort of pick your brain about how to build a career in this industry, and get some of your insight into market trends and growth opportunities.

Thank you so much for your time and I hope to hear from you soon. My cell phone number is [ ], and my e-mail address is [something professional—not BusinessManager@LennyDykstra .com].

Sincerely,

[You]

There are a few things that are great about this letter and will give it a very good shot at success:

1. You're writing to the CEO of a six-unit restaurant chain that received media attention for its growth. This means that the company probably isn't so big that the guy won't have time to respond to you—but it's growing, which means that they are probably in hiring mode.

2. You're not asking for anything other than a phone call and some career advice and thoughts on the industry—which will give you a chance to impress him and may lead him to think about trying to hire you. This is the opposite dynamic of most job interviews, and it puts you in a better position.

3. By noting that you read about him in a trade magazine, you immediately identify yourself as someone who is serious about the industry. How many recent college grads do you think are reading trade magazines? I can guarantee it's a much lower percentage than the number who are filling out online job applications, and that alone makes it a worthwhile strategy.

4. Even if the guy isn't hiring, there is no harm in getting to know the hotshot CEO of a growing company in the field you want to be in. It may lead to other things, or come in handy down the road.

5. If it is a restaurant CEO you're contacting—and even if it isn't—you could at least wind up getting a free lunch.

A word of warning about this: It's a numbers game. You won't get responses to every hotshot you reach out to. But you only need one.

Another great thing to do is to reach out to professional organizations in your area—and just tell them that you're new to the industry and looking for advice and guidance. These groups are great because their reason for existing is to help.

Spend less time filling out endless numbers of online job applications, and devote your energy to making human connections instead. That's the career approach that's worked for me, a Tony award-winning composer, and countless others. It can work for you too if you have a sincere passion for your field and a willingness to read and think and write instead of just hitting "send." And if you don't have a sincere passion for something, you are going to have a lot of trouble with your career *and* your happiness.

Attending networking events is also a hugely important part of kick-starting a career. Almost regardless of what career you're interested in, there is a professional association within your state that has events, panel discussions, lunches, seminars, and conferences. These can be fantastic places to learn about trends in the industry and make connections with people in a way that you just can't when you're spending all of your time filling out online job applications.

How to Negotiate a Salary

I am an expert on negotiation; I own *Jerry Maguire* on VHS and have watched it *seven* times.

There's an important caveat about discussions of salary for recent graduates in this economy and the economy that we're likely to be in for the foreseeable future: This is probably not the time for hardball negotiating tactics, and you probably don't have much leverage.

If you're looking at entry-level-type jobs, the room for negotiating for a higher salary is probably limited to looking a little sad when you hear the offer and hesitating before saying yes. If you're lucky, that awkward look (that says, "How will I ever be able to pay my rent? But I'm way too grateful to ask for more") and those two or three seconds of silence will be met with a sweetener of some kind. Otherwise, just suck it up and say yes. Do a great job and earn raises once you've become deeply loved and indispensable. As I write this, there are seven people seeking work for every job opening, and little evidence that this is likely to change dramatically anytime soon.[6]

Your best bet is to present yourself as being as differentiated and as valuable as you can before you even start the interview; get them excited about the prospect of hiring you, and inspire them to make an "end of conversation" offer—a deal that they know is a little higher than you're likely to receive elsewhere—because they just don't want to take the risk of losing you.

In the long run, if you're young enough to be reading this, your earnings will have a lot more to do with your performance than your salary at your first job. The average grad stays at his or her first full-time job for only 1.6 years at which point—knowing you as I do, someone will be bidding high to entice you to leave your current job (a position of strength from which to negotiate) and come work for them.[7]

Be long-term greedy, not short-term greedy. The money you make in your first years in the workforce is a tiny fraction of your long-term trajectory. Here are some things to keep in mind:

Don't give a salary range too quickly, and don't feel obligated to disclose how much you earned at your previous job. The application might ask for salary requirements or current salary. I recommend just writing in "negotiable" or better yet, "TBD" or "N/A" or "TTYL" or "NYFB," because very few people have the self-confidence to argue with acronyms. The general rule is that the first person to mention a number is in a weak position. If the recruiter or employer asks you about your salary expectations during the interview, I recommend creating a diversion. "OH MY GOODNESS!" you might say, staring out the window. "IS THAT HALLEY'S COMET?!?!?" Or you could spill something. Seriously, though: sometimes it's unavoidable, in which case you should just be honest and pick as broad of a range as you can.

Show, don't tell. If you're a computer programmer and someone is advertising for a freelance computing job, show him or her work that you've done that's similar. If you're applying for a job that requires physical strength, lift the interviewer's desk over your head.

Know what's fair. Just as you want to know what comparable houses are selling for when you're looking at real estate, you want to get an idea of the salary range for the job you're taking so you can determine whether the offer is a complete lowball or something that is within the expected range. You can view government data for salaries in all different fields based on location by visiting www.bls.gov/bls/blswage.htm or GlassDoor.com. It's unclear how reliable this data is, but it's still worth checking.

How We're Perceived in the Workplace

All that stands between the graduate and the top of the ladder is the ladder.

—ANONYMOUS

When you go into a job interview—or your first day on the job—as a member of Gen Y, you have a huge advantage: The people who work there think you're lazy, selfish, narcissistic, and basically useless.

Why is this good? Because it gives you an opportunity to instantly—and very effectively—prove that you're better than that, which will help you stand out from the other people in your age group applying for the same job.

Ramit Sethi of IWillTeachYoutoBeRich.com calls this "the Craigslist penis effect." According to Sethi, any woman who posts an ad on the personals section of Craigslist will instantly be bombarded with creeps sending her nude photos of themselves, but a guy who logs onto the site and replies to a woman's ad with a halfway civilized response will automatically seem, by comparison, to be a wonderful guy. Ramit says that the Craigslist penis effect describes scenarios "where everyone else is so horrible that, by being even half-decent, you can dominate everyone else and win."[8] By coming off as a modest, hard worker who doesn't feel entitled, you'll instantly stand out from the bulk of our generation.

In his book *Not Everyone Gets a Trophy: How to Manage Generation Y*, human resources expert Bruce Tulgan recounts the story of a twenty-five-year-old applying for a job at a health care consulting firm. During the interview, he casually asked this question: "You should know that surfing is really important to me and there might be days when the surf's really up. Would you mind if I came in a little later on those days?"

These stories are emblematic of the stereotypes about Gen Y workers. Remember: Leonardo da Vinci had to carve a lot of jack-o'-lanterns and Dollar Tree figurines before he got to carve *David*.[9]

Just how bad is our reputation? Take a look:

- In a survey that asked people to define themselves in terms of their generation's most important traits, Gen Yers defined themselves in terms of technology use, pop culture, and tolerance; Gen Yers were just as likely to define themselves in terms of clothes as in terms of work ethic. Among older generations, work ethic was at least twice as popular as a defining characteristic.[10]

- Gen Yers are generally overconfident about their futures. In 1999, teens predicted that they would be earning an average of $75,000 per year by age thirty. The average thirty-year-old earned just $27,000 that year. Employers see this as evidence of entitlement.

- A 2008 survey of 2,500 hiring managers found that 87 percent agreed that younger workers "feel more entitled in terms of compensation, benefits, and career advancement than older workers." Younger workers are also less likely to agree with the statement that "a worker should do a decent job whether or not his supervisor is around." Industrial workers in 2006 were only willing to lift 69 percent as much as industrial workers in 1991. Students in 2006 were also less willing to work overtime than students in 1976.

Fast Company reporter Keith Hammonds summed it up this way: "Most achievers don't work hard just at work. They think about their work a lot of the time outside the office. Even if they acknowledge the value of paying attention to their families or their health, they're consumed—and thrilled—by the task at hand."[11]

No amount of passion can substitute for paying your dues. Indeed, in most fields, there will be—especially at the beginning—work that isn't fulfilling. But as long as your work is on a path to self-actualization, you'll have the feeling of momentum that will make it possible to stay focused.

If you want to be successful in your career, you will have to make sacrifices. There's nothing inherently wrong with wanting to have a lame career where you just scrape by and leave at five each day in order to get home and watch the Food Network. But if you put a high value on having a "balanced" life at the beginning of your career *and* want to be highly successful, you are setting yourself up for disappointment. This is why it's so important to find something you find fulfilling. As the saying goes, do work you love and never work a day in your life.

Hey, If I Wanted to Learn, I Woulda Gone to Grad School

The reality of the world right now is that you're probably not going to be able to get anything resembling your dream job, but you need to find something that will pay the bills and you can parlay that into your dream job later.

There are no meaningless jobs when you need money. And a seemingly meaningless job might very well lead you to the opportunity or passion that will make your career. You just never know.

When George Bodenheimer graduated from Denison University in Ohio with an economics degree in 1980, he wrote a letter to an upstart cable network called ESPN and managed to talk his way into an interview.

"He looked at my résumé and said I was qualified to be a driver," he recalled in an interview for the book *Those Guys Have All the Fun*. "Then he asked me if I would mind shoveling snow. I said, 'Not if you tell me where you keep your shovel.'

"My dad . . . gave me some great advice that I always mention to kids looking for work," he remembered. "He said, 'If you think sports-television business would be a good career, then if they call you, you should accept the job. It doesn't matter what the pay is or what the job is. You should make a career decision, not a money decision.'"[12]

Today, Bodenheimer still works at ESPN, but now he's the president of the company. As billionaire Mark Cuban says, "Whatever your hobbies, interests, passions are, find the ones you love the best and GET A JOB in the business that supports it. It could be as a clerk, a salesperson, whatever you can find. You have to start learning the business somewhere. Instead of paying to go to school somewhere, you are getting paid to learn. It may not be the perfect job, but there is no perfect path to getting rich."[13]

Why You Need a Side Job

There is a lot to be said for throwing yourself 110 percent into your job. But for some people and in some situations, another strategy can make sense: Just as diversification is important in the world of investing, it's also generally not a bad idea to have a bit of diversification in your career. Entrepreneurship and freelancing are generally seen as risky endeavors, but there is at least as much risk in being completely dependent on one employer, especially in a world where most people can be laid off at a moment's notice with little or nothing in the way of severance?

Meet Stephanie O'Dea, bestselling author and founder of the one-million-page-views-per-month blog *A Year of Slow Cooking* (http://crockpot365.blogspot.com).

"Multiple streams of income, especially in this economy, are important," she says. "You can't put all your eggs in one basket." That, combined with the fact that she had three young children, is what inspired O'Dea to start blogging after she came up with the idea as a joke at a party with her husband.

"I had had too much wine at New Year's and I said, 'I should do a Crockpot blog!'" she told me.

"I married my high school sweetheart and before having kids, I ran preschool centers. Because of that, I kind of knew right away that when we were going to have children, I wanted to find a way to be their primary caretaker," she says. "That was my primary goal in seeing if I could get the crockpot site to earn some money."

My goal here is not to suggest that everyone run out and start a blog about some obscure corner of the world. As side gigs go, starting a blog is a tough one because in most cases it will be a long time before you have the traffic built to the point where it's profitable, and most blogs never reach that point.

But when you're looking for ways to earn a side income, starting with a passion is a fantastic way to go. Even adding just a few hundred dollars per month to your income can be a financial freedom life changer—and if that side job is something you're passionate about, it could mushroom into a new career that replaces a day job that doesn't excite you.

Here are some popular (though not necessarily great) ways to earn extra money on the side:

Elance.com. This is sort of the career equivalent of going to singles night at a really dive bar; there are opportunities to be had, but it's definitely a meat market. Basically, you can post your résumé and, more important, you can browse freelance jobs that are posted in everything from writing to editing to video work to Web design. You can offer proposals and see whether you get hired. It's a big business. Since inception, Elance.com has brought together freelancers and employers for more than $390 million in projects.

Bartending. If you're hot and can get a gig just Friday and Saturday nights when you're free and they're busy, you can make big tips *and* not spend money yourself those nights. And it's fun—you're the star.

Multilevel marketing. Stay away from this one. These are companies that sell supplements, household products, sex toys (seriously), and pretty much anything else through networks of distributors. In most cases though, the money is made through recruiting *other* salespeople rather than through the sale of products, and critics charge that these businesses resemble pyramid schemes. Many of them also have a really creepy cultlike atmosphere to them. A few are ethical—like Avon—but for the most part, there are better ways to make money on the side.

Ramit Sethi's Earn1K program. I almost never recommend expensive online courses. But I know Ramit, and he's the real deal. His Earn1K program is real, and will help you develop an idea for a side business and carry it through to fruition. It comes with a money-back guarantee, but it does cost $1,000. You should consider this program only after you are debt-free and have a little bit of money in savings; in fact, Ramit doesn't accept anyone into this program who has too much debt. To get a free sample of the material and perhaps sign up, visit Earn1K.com.

Etsy.com. If you're a crafter—you weave baskets or hammer hubcaps into sculpture—this can be a fantastic site to sell your wares on. The average earnings for Etsy sellers are only in the hundreds, but people with distinctive products are occasionally able to earn a living from the site.

Fiverr.com. This site is hilarious. Basically, you post an ad (which is free) for a task that you will perform for $5— Fiverr.com keeps $1 of that as its commission and you get the other $4. Tasks that people buy on Fiverr can include everything from proofreading a résumé to recording a video singing "Happy Birthday" to giving Spanish lessons on Skype or drawing a caricature. My favorite is the guy who earns a decent amount of money recording videos of himself crying hysterically about whatever his patron wants him to. There's another guy who promises "an emotional rant for $5." He has tons of positive feedback, meaning that he actually is making money with this. And another great part of the site is that it can help you make connections doing tiny jobs for clients who, if you impress them, may keep coming back to you or refer you to others.

Craigslist.org. You probably know this site already, but it really is a fantastic place to find short-term freelance-type jobs that will generate some cash. Be careful of scams, though. Avoid anything that is full of hype and only work with people who are local. Be very skeptical of anything that is commission based. With these kind of jobs, you want to be paid guaranteed money for your time.

Starting Your Own Business

I was once on Sean Hannity's radio show, taking calls from people in search of financial advice, when a guy called in saying he wanted to start a restaurant but didn't have enough capital to do it, and he wanted to know what the best way to go about borrowing the mo—

And that was where I cut him off. Because anytime anyone asks me about the best way to borrow money for anything other than real estate, I automatically cut him or her off. It's involuntary, like acid reflux.

My answer to him was basically this: Wanting to own your own business is a great goal, but it's a goal that's best financed without debt. I know, there's no way to start a restaurant without debt—or waiting years until you've saved a ton of money. But what about starting your own catering company? You can buy the supplies you need for very little money if you buy them used, start advertising on Craigslist, and get referrals through friends and family. Then you can hire temporary help just for the days you have events and you won't have to quit your day job if you limit yourself to events on weekends to start. No big rent, no over-budget renovations, no nightmarish delays getting the liquor license that's your only hope of making a profit—and yet if the catering business succeeds, you might amass the capital to start a restaurant after all, and the reputation to attract a clientele—and people who like the food at your restaurant might want you to cater their next party, and pretty soon you're going to be the richest man or woman in town, with your own cooking show on TLC, a bestselling cookbook, and your own bestselling line of gourmet ketchup—without ever having had to borrow a dime. See how easy this is?

If you have a business idea, chances are it's a big idea. But try to think of a way to start smaller. Want to start a clothing store? Maybe you could start by setting up a personal styling business, giving your friends free makeovers to build a portfolio of photographs to advertise your services.

As Dave Ramsey recently tweeted, "60 percent of all small businesses needed less than $5,000 to get started."[14] Also, I just footnoted a tweet.

Should I Continue My Education Past College?

One of the most challenging career-oriented decisions involves the question of whether to pursue further education beyond the bachelor's degree.

I'm at a little bit of a disadvantage on this topic because I couldn't wait to graduate college. I wasn't particularly proud, or relieved that I had managed to finish; I was just glad that I didn't have to study for tests anymore, or sit in a class with a bunch of Anime freaks learning about medieval churches with a professor who needed a hockey puck-size Prozac.

So I have a hard time relating to people who are just incredibly excited about the prospect of spending a few more years taking classes and writing papers that no one will ever read except a professor whose primary qualification for teaching is that he or she has written *a lot* of papers that no one ever read.

But there are a few good reasons to go to grad school:

> **Your employer will pay for it.** If your employer will pay for you to further your education, and it's something you want to do. . . . Duhhhh!
>
> **It will provide you with a credential that is necessary for a very specific career path you want to pursue.** If you want to get a particular job and having a certain degree will give you a leg up, go for it. Just make sure you can afford it.

You are debt-free and will be able to pay cash. If you are debt-free and able to pay cash to further your education, then you have my blessing; just make sure you won't derive more benefit from doing something else with the money.

So those are all the good reasons to go to grad school. But there are also many bad reasons to go to grad school, and the business that is higher education won't tell you about them because, let's face it: they have bills to pay and they need your money.

The love of learning. Get over it. As Matt Damon says in *Good Will Hunting*, "You dropped a hundred and fifty grand on a **** education you coulda got for a dollah fifty in late chahges at the public library." And that was before Google. Now you can even save the dollah fifty.

The economy is bad. Sure it is. But taking on a huge amount of debt won't make it better. If your career troubles will end with the beginning of a new economic cycle, your best bet is probably to hunker down, work at whatever minimum wage job you can find, and avoid accruing more debt. As one career expert told me, no one is going to hold the fact that you work at a grocery store during a recession against you. Human resources people know how bad the job market is, and they'll understand that you did what you had to do.

Can't get a job. This is the "higher education as Nigerian e-mail scam" approach. You enrolled in undergrad because you were told it would get you a job and then the higher-education system comes back with "Dear Gentle Sir or Madam, There has been a small problem in processing your payment. Please wire an additional $5,000 to us to finance foreign stamp tax tariffs, and we will deposit $25 million into your account presently." At some point, you've gotta realize you got scammed and cut your losses. If you can't figure out what you are going to do with your life, grad school is a *really* expensive place to try to figure it out. And if you're underemployed, working part-time as a fry cook at McDonald's, and are tired of your friends in law school asking you what you're doing with your life, just tell them you made $80,000 this year—$10,000 working as a fry cook and $70,000 by not going to law school.

Prestige and ego. This is my all-time least favorite reason for going to grad school—and, I'm afraid, it's also one of the most popular. One guy who was planning to borrow $100,000 to pursue a law degree from Western New England University told me that he wanted the "power and respect" that comes from being a lawyer. "I want to be able to say 'I am a licensed attorney!'" he told me. Wicked lame. But maybe I just feel that way because I don't have a law degree.

You have an unrealistic career goal. This is a really, really awkward thing to talk about in a world of positive thinking and a "You can be anything you want to be!" mentality. But you need to research how realistic your career goal is before you spend a ton of time and money pursuing it. According to *Scientific American*, there's a PhD glut in the sciences (and by the way, it's worse in the humanities). "[F]ew young PhDs can get started on the career for which their graduate education purportedly trained them, namely, as faculty members in academic research institutions," the magazine reported. "In fact, however, only about 25 percent of those earning American science PhDs will ever land a faculty job that enables them to apply for the competitive grants that support academic research. And even fewer—15 percent by some estimates—will get a post at the kind of research university where the nation's significant scientific work takes place."[15] In other words: I'm sorry to say this, but unless you have an unlimited amount of money or have graduated at the top of your class in everything you've ever done and won multiple top awards for every paper you've ever written, furthering your education with the goal of teaching at the college level is probably unwise. Before you pursue further education, look at Bureau of Labor statistics for your hoped-for field, and talk to people who are in the industry. Find out whether you're likely to find an opening.

To defer student loans. There's a disturbing trend of recent grads with excessive student loan debt enrolling in grad school in order to avoid having to start making payments. Like racking up *more* debt will really help. This is so dumb as to not even merit my ordinarily copious sarcasm.

Now that we've covered all that, let's talk about the ways to pay for grad school and some traps to watch out for:

Student loans. As someone who got his start telling people never to borrow for an undergraduate degree, it pains me to say this, but, if you want to become a doctor and have the ability to make it through medical school, often it's not possible to do it debt-free. This is, incidentally, a big part of why I'm so insistent that people not borrow at all for undergrad— to preserve their borrowing power in case they want to pursue a graduate or professional degree (see my first book, *Debt-Free U*, for more on this). But outside of law school and medical school, you really shouldn't be borrowing. A master's degree in social work, for example, costs far less money, and you should be able to get a teaching assistant position and/or a part-time job to allow you to cash flow it. Another rule: Before you borrow for further education, buckle down and pay off all your loans from your undergraduate degree. If that's not a realistic option for you, it means you already have too much student loan debt and need to come up with a life plan that doesn't involve taking on more.

Be extremely careful about scholarships that require you to maintain a certain GPA. The *New York Times* recently reported on a major scandal in law school scholarship programs. Many prominent programs offer significant grants to anyone who maintains a GPA over, say, 3.5, but then they adjust their curves so that almost everyone falls just short of that GPA.[16] In anything other than higher education, this would be considered fraud.

Military service. The commitments and risks associated with military service are too great to be assumed solely based on the promise of help with paying for education. But if military service is something you're thinking about, you should know that there are phenomenal educational benefits associated with it. Talk to a military recruiter to find out more.

Law School

Law school, which was once the surefire, can't-lose ticket to prestige and a high salary, has come under scrutiny in recent years as more and more grads are living to regret their decision to pursue a Juris Doctor.

In 2006, the *Wall Street Journal* reported on the huge divide between grads of top law schools and everyone else: "[T]he mean salary for graduates of top 10 law schools is $135,000 while it is $60,000 for 'tier three' schools. It's certainly possible that tier-three graduates tend to gravitate toward lower-paying public-interest and government jobs, but this lower salary may also reflect the nonlegal nature of many of these jobs and the fact that these graduates are settling for anything that will pay the bills."[17]

The hard reality is this: Unless you have the chops to get into a top law school, the investment of time and money—especially if it's debt-financed—that comes from pursuing a law degree is highly unlikely to make it a good investment. More likely, it will be a high-risk land mine. Law school just isn't the investment it once was, and most people should steer clear. I know this stinks if you really want to be a lawyer, but think back to Jon Acuff's advice: "A lawyer is a position." If you're passionate about the idea of being a lawyer, try to think of an alternative career that doesn't require such tremendous financial risk with very poor odds of a good payoff.

CONCLUSION

Ya Done!

I hope that the material in this book will be of help to people, as well as Khloe Kardashian. I also hope that the presentation—no charts, no graphs, and only one math problem that involved calculating 2,000 years of compound interest—assuaged any fears you might have had about money being too complicated. For the checklist crowd, I've distilled my money philosophy down to a few key points, although they are not numbered, because whenever someone sends me a numbered list of ideas I immediately assume that he or she is full of crap:

- **Materialism killed the dinosaurs.** OK, not really. But materialism is really, really bad and will lead to misery and poverty in your life and will also have a negative impact on the rest of the world. Anything that you can do to combat a consumer culture that encourages materialism will improve your own life and the world. Your life will not be better because it has more stuff in it.
- **Debt will make your life bad.** Debt adds stress, uncertainty, and risk to your life. Certain debts are worth it—but mortgages and maybe medical school loans are the only ones I can think of. Car loans are usually accepted as a fact of life, but they don't have to be and your life will be better without them.

- **A little bit of money in savings will make life good.** Most personal finance experts recommend a six- to eight-month emergency fund; that's a fantastic goal and something that everyone should strive for. But even having enough cash so that a toilet malfunction or flat tire doesn't lead to major financial stress makes a huge difference. Strive to have a couple thousand dollars in a savings account at all times, and then try to build up to more.

- **Keep your fixed costs low.** It's one thing to have expensive habits: In tough times, you can always dial back on them. But when you start to amass stuff like big mortgages, car payments, student loans, and credit card payments, you lose flexibility in your life. Flexibility and freedom will make you happy.

- **Bad people work in the financial services industry.** Don't trust bankers, car salespeople, or the financial experts you see on TV. There are some good people who choose to go into this line of work—but they're a minority.

- **Simplicity, laziness, and inattentiveness are the keys to investing success.** Investing is not like most endeavors: Beyond a very basic level, you can't increase your odds of success by learning more and working harder. Buying and holding index mutual funds in tax-deferred and tax-free accounts is the ticket to investment success. The more attention you pay to the day-to-day and month-to-month fluctuations in your accounts, the harder it will be to stick to your long-term plan. So invest automatically each month, and then go do something else.

- **Eat brown rice.** It's affordable, easy to cook, and much better for you than the processed, simple carbs that people load into their diets. It also helps prevent you from becoming pear-shaped.

- **Your career should excite you.** Remember: This is the number one predictor of life happiness. The decision to scale back expenses to do something you're passionate about is unlikely to be a decision you'll regret.

So there ya have it. Seventy thousand words consisting of every-thing that I know about money; I actually ran out of material at around 65,000, so there's a good 5,000 words of content here that is not, strictly speaking, true, but I spread it throughout the book to try to minimize the impact. Sorry for any inconvenience, including but not limited to an IRS audit, a $15,000 heating bill, or food poisoning. A small price to pay, I hope you'll agree, for being smarter, richer, and less pear-shaped (see brown rice, previous page) than your parents. God love 'em.

NOTES

INTRODUCTION

1. Drentea, P., and P. J. Lavrakas. (2000). "Over the Limit: The Association Among Health, Race, and Debt." *Social Science and Medicine*. 50(4): 517–29
2. Kasser, T. (2011). "Can Thrift Bring Happiness?" *Social and Personality Psychology Compass*. 5(11): 865–77.
3. www.frbsf.org/publications/community/review/vol5_issue3/choi.pdf +effects+of+debt+stress&hl=en&gl=us&pid=bl&srcid=ADGEESj0FZf0 zlfa-Xvkj5PfIzKFyQc-dyyvR4XU9Q7SjEtYlZrgKMcVCrsaBuApRqN NslfRk3hGCgflaW0BFE8cs37vfZGThpfFf9ebeDxFl-NyJG 0sRO5xNIrQ4p_HXnckBttNsmhB&sig=AHIEtbTsAmzhlGhYpsQhVw CT-q_A0lG6tw
4. http://www.worldatwork.org/waw/adimComment?id=28631

CHAPTER 1

1. http://www.zimbio.com/BravoTV/articles/182/REAL+HOUSEWIVES +ATLANTA+Sheree+Whitfield+Forced
2. http://articles.ocregister.com/2009-06-09/housing/24588070_1_loan -modification-default-notices
3. http://bumpshack.com/2009/08/11/lisa-wu-hartwell-real-housewife-of -atlanta-foreclosure-photos/
4. http://www.housingwatch.com/2010/08/31/real-housewife-averts -foreclosure-on-o-c-home/
5. http://news-briefs.ew.com/2010/11/18/real-housewives-of-new-york-city-star -files-for-bankruptcy/
6. http://www.thedailybeast.com/articles/2011/07/31/heidi-montag-spencer -pratt-on-plastic-surgery-the-hills-reality-tv.html
7. Ryan, L., and S. Dziurawiec. (2001). "Materialism and its relationship to life satisfaction." *Social Indicators Research*. 55(2): 185–97.
8. http://www.csmonitor.com/Business/2010/1220/You-bought-it-Are-you-happy
9. http://www.forbes.com/2004/09/21/cx_mh_0921happiness.html
10. http://s.psych.uiuc.edu/~ediener/Documents/Pursuit.Happ.scientific %20american.pdf

11. http://blogs.wsj.com/wealth/2011/01/12/whos-buying-all-that-luxury-not -the-rich/

12. http://www.acrwebsite.org/topic.asp?artid=351

13. Craker, L. *Money Secrets of the Amish*. Nashville, TN: Thomas Nelson, 2011, p. 96.

14. http://latimesblogs.latimes.com/technology/2008/08/iphone-i-am-ric.html

15. TinyURL.com/Zac-Music

16. tinyurl.com/Zac-Burpee

17. Craker, *Money Secrets*, p. 103.

18. Baumeister, R., and J. Tierney. *Willpower: Rediscovering the Greatest Human Strength*. New York: Penguin Press, 2011, p. 17.

19. http://www.boston.com/news/local/massachusetts/articles/2009/09/02/bu _dorm_offers_a_study_in_luxury/?page=2

CHAPTER 2

1. Bogle, J. *Enough: True measures of money, business, and life*. Hoboken, NJ: John Wiley and Sons, Inc., 2009, p. 35.

2. tinyurl.com/Zac-FICO

3. http://www.insure.com/car-insurance/most-and-least-expensive-states-2010 .html

4. http://www.walletpop.com/2011/01/31/credit-bureau-starts-tracking-rent -payments-good-news-or-bad-ne/

5. http://www.smartmoney.com/spend/family-money/4-reasons-to-forgo-credit -monitoring-services-23454/

6. http://www.iwillteachyoutoberich.com/credit-card-perks/

7. http://www.creditcards.com/credit-card-news/credit-card-industry-facts -personal-debt-statistics-1276.php

8. The Proprietary 15-Year Longitudinal North American Credit Card Use Survey at the Zac Institute for Just Checking to Make Sure You're Reading His Footnotes

9. http://www.credit.com/blog/2010/11/when-using-plastic-consumers-spend -more/

10. http://www.jstor.org/pss/2489426

11. http://www.cbsnews.com/stories/2011/07/30/earlyshow/saturday /main20085803.shtml

12. http://blogs.smartmoney.com/paydirt/2011/05/26/the-trouble-with -redeeming-air-miles/

13. http://www.sciencedaily.com/releases/2010/10/101018174345.htm

14. http://www.binghamton.edu/magazine/index.php/magazine/feature/can -credit-cards-make-you-fat

15. http://moneywatch.bnet.com/saving-money/blog/so-money/save-money
    -dump-the-dollar-bill/1557/
16. http://www.timesrecordnews.com/news/2009/jun/07/family-pet-gets-credit
    -card-job-offers-in-mail/
17. http://www.creditcards.com/credit-card-news/credit-card-industry-facts
    -personal-debt-statistics-1276.php
18. http://www.daveramsey.com/article/the-basics-of-your-debit-card/
    lifeandmoney_creditcards/text1/
19. http://blogs.wsj.com/economics/2011/05/23/nearly-half-of-americans-are
    -financially-fragile/
20. http://www.king5.com/news/125105599.html
21. http://www.clevelandfed.org/research/commentary/2011/2011-13.cfm
22. http://articles.moneycentral.msn.com/Investing/Extra/customer-service
    -hall-of-shame-companies-2010.aspx
23. http://www.insurance.com/auto-insurance/saving-money/does-your
    -occupation-affect-your-auto-insurance-rate.aspx
24. http://bucks.blogs.nytimes.com/2011/05/30/tempted-to-speed-consider-your
    -auto-insurance/
25. http://articles.moneycentral.msn.com/Insurance/InsureYourCar/which-cars
    -cost-more-or-less-to-insure.aspx
26. http://motherjones.com/politics/2011/04/gary-rivlin-tax-prep-refund
    -anticipation-loan
27. http://www.nytimes.com/2009/09/26/your-money/health-insurance/
    26money.html
28. http://www.newsweek.com/2010/06/03/treasury-now-accepts-credit-card
    -donations-to-help-pay-the-national-debt.html

CHAPTER 3

1. http://www.dailyfinance.com/2011/01/02/finance-boosting-and-savings-tips
   -for-2011/
2. http://www.daveramsey.com/article/the-truth-about-bankruptcy/

CHAPTER 4

1. http://www.usinflationcalculator.com/uncategorized/12-days-of-christmas
   -items-now-total-86609/1000281
2. Weston, L. *The Ten Commandments of Money.* New York: Hudson Street
   Press, 2011, p. 44.
3. Goldie, D., and G. Murray. *The Investment Answer.* New York: Business Plus,
   2011, p. 12.

4. http://www.marketwatch.com/story/women-are-better-investors-and-heres
-why-2011-06-14

5. http://www.examiner.com/city-buzz-in-los-angeles/stock-market-gyrates
-from-libyan-oil-crisis

6. http://money.cnn.com/video/markets/2011/07/29/mkts_debt_gdp_selloff
.cnnmoney/

7. http://www.marketwatch.com/story/bottoming-is-a-messy-process
-2011-08-19

8. http://www.marketoracle.co.uk/Article6870.html

9. http://money.usnews.com/money/blogs/capital-commerce/2009/01/27
/10-reasons-to-nix-the-stimulus-plan

10. http://online.wsj.com/article/0,,SB112190164023291519,00.html

11. http://www.getrichslowly.org/blog/2008/06/10/why-it-pays-to-ignore
-financial-news/

12. http://www.cnbc.com/id/44020078

13. http://www.usatoday.com/money/industries/banking/2010-10-19
-islamicbank19_ST_N.htm

CHAPTER 5

1. http://www.us.am.joneslanglasalle.com/Lists/ExpertiseInAction
/Attachments/255/JLL-Gen-Y-Mall-Retailing.pdf

2. Schor, J. *Born to Buy: The Commercialized Child and the New Consumer
Culture.* New York: Scribner, 2005, p. 27.

3. Schor, J. *The Overspent American: Why We Want What We Don't Need.* New
York: Harper Collins, 1999, p. 86.

4. Benson, A. *To Buy or Not to Buy: Why We Overshop and How to Stop.* Boston:
Trumpeter Books, 2008, p. 2.

5. Schor, *Overspent American.* p. 70.

6. Schor, *Overspent American.* p. 48.

7. http://www.smartmoney.com/spending/deals/why-men-should-shop-alone
-1295028816876/

8. http://moneywatch.bnet.com/saving-money/blog/so-money/money-problems
-blame-the-internet/2392/

9. http://www.psychologytoday.com/blog/compulsive-acts/201108/the-great
-recession-our-virtual-lives

10. http://www.wine-economics.org/journal/content/Volume3/number1
/Full%20Texts/01_wine%20economics_Robin%20Goldstein_vol%203
_1.pdf

11. http://www.bitesizeidea.com/bsi/overcome-americas-fixation-with-experts
-ignore-them-and-become-one

12. http://consumerist.com/2011/03/study-kids-think-cereal-with-cartoon
    -mascot-tastes-better.html

13. http://newsfeed.time.com/2011/04/04/the-fashionistas-were-right-designer
    -labels-might-really-improve-your-life/?xid=rss-topstories&utm_source
    =feedburner&utm_medium=feed&utm_campaign=Feed:+time/topstories
    +%28TIME:+Top+Stories%29&utm_content=Google+Reader

14. http://www.housecleaningcentral.com/en/cleaning-tips/clothing/laundry
    -tips.html

15. http://www.ajc.com/lifestyle/living-large-clark-howard-1069079.html

16. http://www.redorbit.com/news/science/51354/study_claims_obese_women
    _earn_30_percent_less/

17. http://www.nytimes.com/2006/12/02/business/02money.html?_r=2&oref
    =slogin&ref=business&pagewanted=print

18. http://www.fitness.gov/mentalhealth.htm

19. http://www.econ.berkeley.edu/~sdellavi/wp/gymemp05-04-20.pdf

20. http://www.engadget.com/2007/06/11/what-kind-of-man-gets-a-zune-tattoo/

21. http://www.consumerreports.org/cro/money/shopping/ways-to-save-on/cell
    -phone-bills/overview/cell-phone-bills.htm

22. http://money.cnn.com/galleries/2010/news/1001/gallery.americas_biggest
    _ripoffs/index.html

23. Weber, L. *In Cheap We Trust: The Story of a Misunderstood American Virtue.*
    New York: Little, Brown and Company, 2009, p. 236.

24. http://www.medicinenet.com/script/main/art.asp?articlekey=52420&page=2

25. http://www.emeraldinsight.com/journals.htm?articleid=857057&show=html

26. http://www.progressivegrocer.com/top-stories/headlines/consumer-insights
    /id32763/shoppers-acting-on-impulse-less-often/

27. http://www.jhsph.edu/publichealthnews/articles/2007/gary_ajpm.html

28. http://forecastchart.com/inflation-food-price.html

29. http://www.walletpop.com/2009/05/08/check-please-beware-this-secret
    -spend-more-trick/

30. http://www.cbsnews.com/8301-503983_162-5217824-503983.html

31. Yeager, J. *The Cheapskate Next Door: The Surprising Secrets of Americans
    Living Happily Below Their Means.* New York: Broadway Books, 2010,
    pp. 29–30.

32. http://fiskeandfreeman.com/AntiquesAsInvestments.aspx

33. Ashwell, R. *Shabby Chic.* New York: Harper Design, 2011, p. 70.

34. Ohrbach, B. M. *A Passion for Antiques.* New York: Clarkson Potter, 2004, p. 30.

35. http://www.lifescript.com/Soul/Self/Well-being/11_Ways_to_Be_Happier
    _This_Year.aspx

36. http://blogs.reuters.com/felix-salmon/2010/01/15/dont-give-money-to-haiti/

37. http://money.cnn.com/2010/10/14/pf/boomerang_kids_move_home/index.htm

CHAPTER 6

1. http://www.edmunds.com/car-buying/confessions-of-a-repo-man.html
2. http://www.investopedia.com/articles/pf/08/cost-car-ownership. asp#axzz1V2ZQIrZk
3. Luhrs, J. *The Simple Living Guide: A Sourcebook for Less Stressful, More Joyful Living.* New York: Broadway Books, 1997, p. 28.
4. http://articles.moneycentral.msn.com/SavingandDebt/SaveonaCar/ ABCsForAGreatCarLoan.aspx
5. http://www.telegraph.co.uk/news/worldnews/asia/japan/1418964/Enjoying -the-smell-of-a-new-car-is-like-glue-sniffing.html
6. Schor, *Overspent American.* p. 57.
7. http://www.nypost.com/p/news/business/luxe_wheels_don_roll_humdrum _worries_CZmVP5JPqyZNGAeG8pkZwM
8. Stanley, T., and W. Danko. *The Millionaire Next Door: Surprising Secrets of America's Wealthy.* New York: Pocket Books, 2000, p. 117.
9. Stanley, T. *Stop Acting Rich . . . And Start Living Like a Real Millionaire.* Hoboken, NJ: John Wiley and Sons, 2009, p. 188.
10. http://www.thomasjstanley.com/blog-articles/268/Stop_Being_Cynical _Look_at_the_Heart.html
11. http://www.consumerreports.org/cro/money/credit-loan/auto-lease-or-buy -4-08/overview/auto-lease-or-buy-ov.htm
12. http://www.edmunds.com/car-buying/drive-a-nearly-new-car-for-almost -free.html?articleid=77147&
13. http://www.wired.com/autopia/2010/07/irv-gordon-2-8-million-mile-volvo/
14. http://www.accessmylibrary.com/coms2/summary_0286-10966010_ITM
15. http://blogs.consumerreports.org/cars/2010/10/2010-annual-car-reliability -survey-best-and-worst-car-types.html
16. http://www.edmunds.com/car-reviews/best-used-cars.html
17. http://www.lendingtree.com/auto-loans/advice/auto-loan-basics/auto -financing-options/

CHAPTER 7

1. http://www.businessweek.com/investor/content/mar2009/pi20090310 _263462.htm
2. http://www.washingtonpost.com/wp-dyn/content/article/2010/04/08/ AR2010040806444.html
3. http://therealdeal.com/newyork/articles/homeowners-outpace-renters-in-net -worth-according-to-the-national-association-of-realtors
4. http://www.truliablog.com/2011/02/09/q1-2011-american-dream-survey/

5. http://finance.fortune.cnn.com/2011/05/25/winners-of-the-rental-economy
/?iid=HP_Highlight
6. http://www.startribune.com/business/117118128.html
7. http://www.dailybusinessreview.com/PubArticleDBR.jsp?id=1202495607948
&hbxlogin=1
8. http://www.ehow.com/how_16570_hedge-against-inflation.html
9. http://extratv.warnerbros.com/2011/06/michael_corbett_can_starbucks
_helo_you_get_a_house_deal.php
10. Luhrs, *The Simple Living* Guide, p. 22.
11. Lasser, J. K., and S. Porter. *Managing Your Money*. New York: Henry Holt
and Co., 1955, p. 154.
12. http://realestate.aol.com/blog/2011/05/09/choosing-a-real-estate-agent
-beware-these-little-white-lies/?fb_ref=article&fb_source=profile_oneline
13. http://online.wsj.com/article/SB10001424052748704655004575113872190094934
.html

CHAPTER 8

1. http://www.usmagazine.com/moviestvmusic/news/jon-gosselin-kate-bank
-account-claim-total-fabrication-2009510
2. http://articles.moneycentral.msn.com/CollegeAndFamily/LoveAndMoney
/why-savers-and-spenders-marry.aspx
3. http://www.salon.com/life/feature/2011/03/09/divorce_finance_opting_out
4. http://news.health.com/2011/06/18/are-men-who-flaunt-flashy-cars-not-the
-marrying-kind/
5. http://www.cbsnews.com/8301-504763_162-20072524-10391704.html
6. http://getcurrency.com/life-style/4-student-loan-mistakes-to-avoid

CHAPTER 9

1. http://www.mcclatchydc.com/2009/06/25/70788/recessions-toll-most-recent
-college.html
2. http://www.christianpost.com/news/new-study-finds-that-depression-rates
-higher-in-affluent-nations-52895/
3. http://www.physorg.com/news70814635.html
4. http://www.alumni.hbs.edu/careers/networking.html
5. http://www.nrn.com/article/burtons-growth-spree?ad=business
6. http://www.ritholtz.com/blog/2011/06/jolts-7-applicants-per-job-opening/
7. http://www.experience.com/corp/load_media_coverage?id=media_coverage
_1166041369638&tab=mc&channel_id=about_us&page_id=media_coverage
_news

8. http://www.iwillteachyoutoberich.com/blog/the-craigslist-penis-effect/

9. Yes, I know Leonardo didn't carve *David*. It was Michelangelo.

10. http://www.dresserassociates.com/blog/what-we-can-learn-from-gen-y
    -about-workkids-say-the-darndest-things/

11. http://www.fastcompany.com/magazine/87/balance-2.html

12. Miller, J. A., and T. Shales. *These Guys Have All the Fun: Inside the World of
    ESPN.* New York: Back Bay Books, 2011, p. 85.

13. http://blogmaverick.com/2011/08/04/how-to-get-rich-2/

14. http://twitter.com/#!/DaveRamsey/status/112277357502533633

15. http://scienceblogs.com/mikethemadbiologist/2010/02/yes_we_have_a_phd
    _glut.php

16. http://www.nytimes.com/2011/05/01/business/law-school-grants.html?_r=2
    &hp=&pagewanted=all

17. http://online.wsj.com/article/SB115103273756588503-search.html

INDEX

Also available from Zac Bissonnette

ISBN 978-1-59184-298-9

"A real mule kick to the high educational status quo."
— *USA Today*

Portfolio/Penguin
A member of Penguin Group (USA) Inc.
www.penguin.com